ORANGE COUNTY PUBLIC SCHOOLS
Purchased with
IASA Title VI Funds

5-98

The Story of Egypt

The Story of Egypt—a **Childcraft** title
(Reg. U.S. Pat. and T.M. Off.—Marca Registrada)

© 1996 World Book, Inc. All rights reserved. This volume may not be reproduced in whole or in part in any form without prior written permission from the publisher.

World Book, Inc.
525 W. Monroe
Chicago, IL 60661

Printed in the USA

ISBN: 0-7166-6457-7

1 2 3 4 5 6 7 8 9 10 99 98 97 96

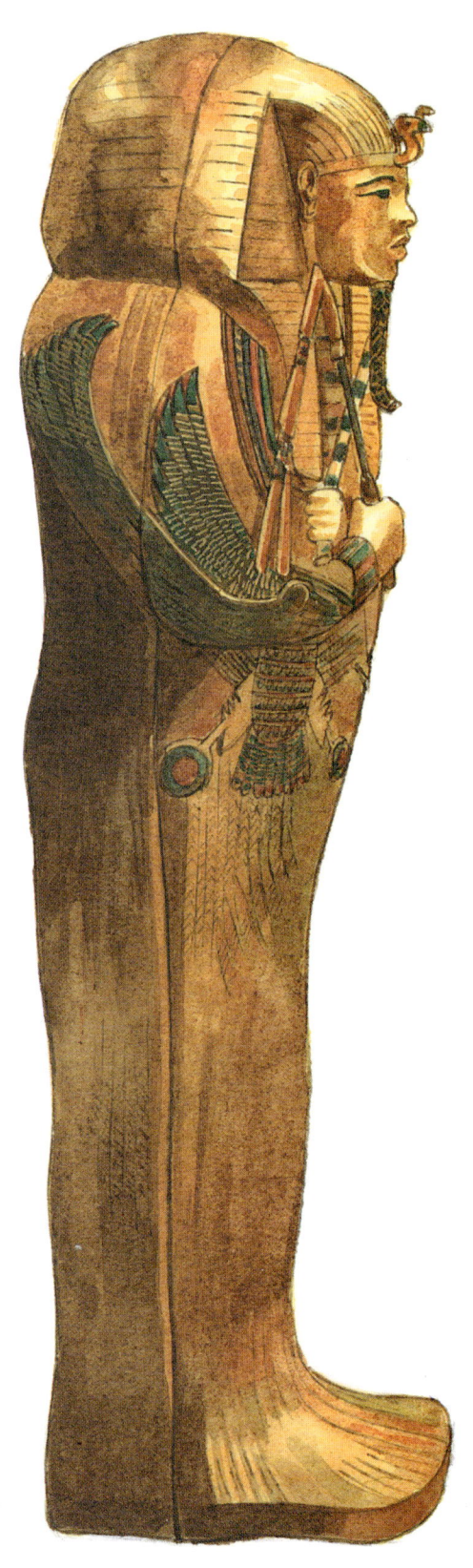

The Story of Egypt

World Book, Inc.
a Scott Fetzer company
Chicago London Sydney Toronto

Consultants:
Mary Kickham Samy
Dept. of English and Comparative Literature
The American University in Cairo
Cairo, Egypt
Member of the Subcommittee on Environmental Education in Egypt

Waheed Samy
Arabic Language Institute
The American University in Cairo
Cairo, Egypt

World Book wishes to thank the following individuals for their contributions to **The Story of Egypt:** Gerry Bailey, Pam Bliss, Donna Cook, Linda Kinnaman, Christine McKenzie, and Janet Russell.

Contents

6   **Predynastic Egypt.**
The life-giving Nile. The first Egyptians. Menes and the beginning of Egyptian civilisation. The first great tombs.

20   **The first kingdoms**
The Old Kingdom. The pyramids. Ancient Egyptian culture. The mummy. The Middle Kingdom and Mentuhotep. The Hyksos rulers.

34   **The Empire**
The great Dynasty XVIII. The warrior pharaohs. Tutankhamen and the discovery of his treasures. Akhenaton and the Amarna Revolution. Ramses the Great.

60   **Alexander and the Ptolemies**
Alexander's conquest of Egypt. The first and last Ptolemies. Cleopatra and her bid to make Egypt great again. The Greek influence. The Roman takeover and Roman culture in Egypt.

74   **The coming of Islam**
The rise of Islam and the story of Muhammad. Egypt becomes a Muslim state. The Crusades and the Kurdish warrior Saladin. The rise of the Mamelukes. Baybars the Panther.

88   **Ottoman Egypt**
Egypt under the Ottomans. The rise of the Ottoman Empire. Exploitation of the people. The tax farmers. Ali Bey and the Mameluke revival. Napoleon and the French invasion. European influence.

96   **Modern Egypt begins**
The reign of Muhammad Ali. Ali's army; his farming and industrial developments. The role of cotton in Egypt's economy. The building of the Suez Canal. The first hints of nationalism.

106   **The British in Egypt**
The British occupation. Egypt's financial problems and the solution. The Aswan Dam. Troubles in Sudan. Khartoum, Kitchener, and the Mahdi. The first Nationalists, Mustafa Kamil. Egypt the protectorate.

126   **After the War**
Egypt becomes a sovereign state. The fear of Zionism and the rise of violent sects like the Muslim Brotherhood.

140   **A Republic**
Egypt ruled by an Egyptian. Egypt the republic. The Suez crisis and its solution. Israel and the wars between it and Egypt. The Camp David Accords. Modern Egypt under Sadat.

Special Words

Index

The river of life

The man looked out across the wide expanse of water that shimmered in the sun. He marvelled at how good the river had always been to him. It had provided him with almost all he needed to live. Without it, he could not exist. The river was, indeed, the river of life, the great and mighty Nile.

Without the Nile River, the longest in Africa, there would be no Egypt. For it was the Nile that provided water to make the fertile valley which, in turn, provided a place for people to settle, grow crops, and feed and water their animals. The river also provided a watery highway for the boats people used to travel and to carry goods.

For thousands of years, the Nile overflowed and deposited rich, black soil along its riverbanks. The fertile soil enabled farmers to produce huge stocks of food.

As the river does today, the ancient Nile began its journey to the sea in Africa. After passing through the granite barrier called the First Cataract, at Aswan, it flowed north through sandstone and then limestone beds that formed cliffs on either side of the river valley. Finally, the river divided into as many as seven branches, although today only two exist. Here soil deposits formed the Nile Delta. The waters of the Nile poured from the Delta into the Mediterranean Sea.

The most important feature of the Nile was the flood, called the *Inundation*, which was caused by rains that fell in central Africa and the Ethiopian Highlands. In early May the river was at its lowest level; then in July the

river would begin to rise quickly. During August it rose even more and slowly spread out, remaining over its banks for several weeks and depositing a thin layer of mud, or silt, over the land. When the floodwaters went down in October, they left a strip of fertile land about 10 kilometres wide on each side of the river. This land was ploughed and seeded by farmers.

The fertile land that the river provided allowed Egypt to prosper and, in time, to develop one of the great civilisations of our world.

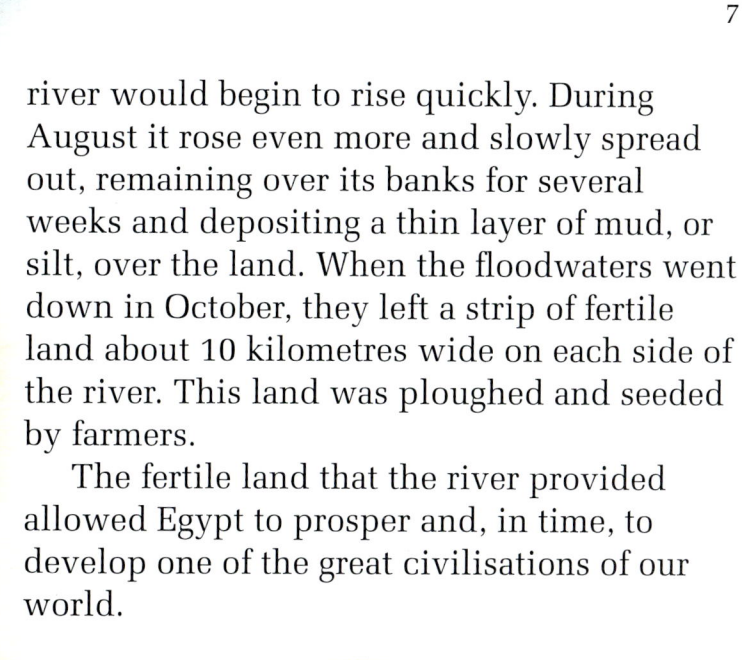

The first Egyptians

The boy watched eagerly as his father delicately chipped at a piece of flint. The flint would soon be worked into a barbed arrowhead that the boy would attach to an arrow shaft. He would use his arrow, and others, with his bow to practice fishing and hunting near his home in the Nile Valley. The boy belonged to one of the first groups of people to live in what we now call Egypt.

The first humans to dwell in the Nile Valley lived by hunting, fishing, and gathering wild plants to eat. There were many more animals than today, and many types of plants grew, as the rainfall was abundant and the Nile was larger than it is now.

The development of civilisation in the Nile Valley began when the nomadic hunter-gatherers were replaced by settled farming, or agricultural, communities. We call these groups of people the Predynastic cultures because they existed just before the great Egyptian dynasties, beginning in about 6000 B.C.

The oldest known northern cultures were at Fayum and Merimda. But in the south, around Badari, a more important group evolved called the Badarian culture. These people kept domestic animals such as oxen, sheep, and goats, but they still hunted and fished as well. They also produced black-topped red pottery and made bone needles, ivory spoons, and sickles.

About 4000 B.C., the Badarians were replaced by the Naqada I culture, which originated at Naqada, north of modern Luxor.

Flint objects were made by *pressure flaking* and grinding. Pressure flaking means that thin slivers of flint were removed from one face of the object to create a delicate, rippled effect. The cutting edge was then sharpened further.

The Naqada I spread through Upper Egypt and became the most important of the Predynastic cultures. Then, about 3600 B.C., came the Naqada II peoples. Their pottery, with lively images of people and animals, distinguishes them from the Naqada I people. At this time, more and more people were living in communities. Clusters of mud-brick dwellings were constructed at the centre of Naqada and also at Hierakonpolis.

The Two Lands

The merchant scraped beads of sweat from his brow as he rested in the shade of a large rock. He had dragged his sled, with its load of pottery, through two villages and had sold practically nothing. If only he could go farther south, where the villages were more prosperous than the ones in his own land of *ta-mehu,* or Lower Egypt. But that was not possible. To the south lay *ta-shema,* or Upper Egypt, and it was not safe to travel there. If only the Two Lands were one, he thought.

In Predynastic times, the peoples of the Nile Valley had gradually formed themselves into two distinct groups, or kingdoms. One was in Upper Egypt, actually the southern part of the valley, and the other was in Lower Egypt, the northern part of the valley, including the Nile Delta. This division of the country, about where Cairo is today, was recognised by the ancient Egyptians themselves, who spoke of their country as the "Two Lands."

The people of the Two Lands lived mainly in small villages. They used the rich soil of the Nile to farm, growing vegetables and probably keeping cattle. They also fished in the Nile for Nile perch.

In time, the kingdom of Upper Egypt began to push northward. The people of the Two Lands warred with each other and, eventually, their conflict led to the unification of Upper and Lower Egypt. Some scholars think the conflict may even have been the basis of the myths of the battles of Horus and Seth, two Egyptian gods.

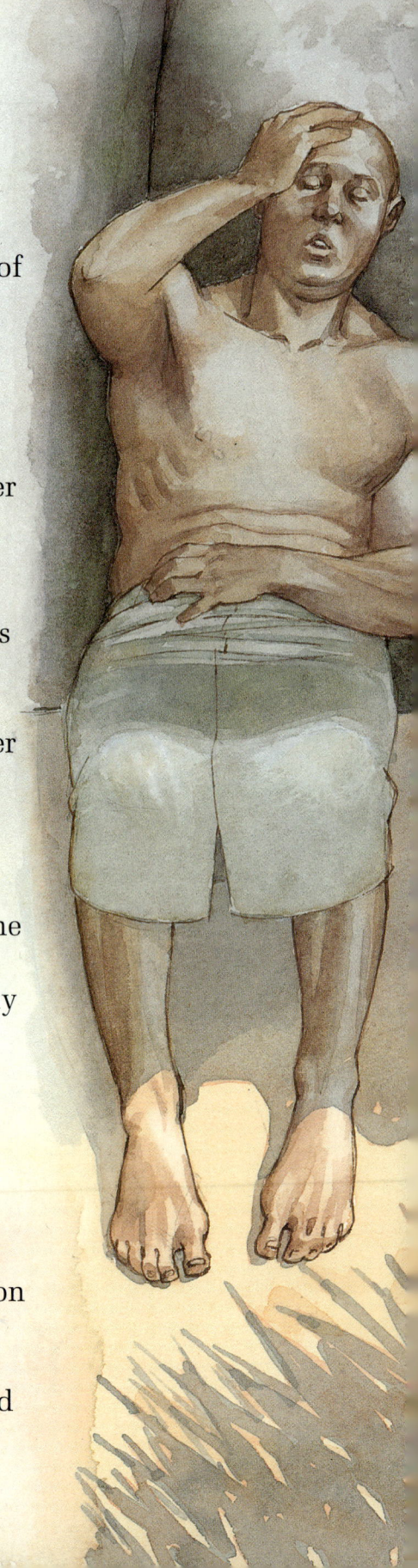

This map shows the areas that became Upper and Lower Egypt.

Horus and Seth

The story of Horus and Seth begins with Seth's murder of the god Osiris, his own brother and the father of Horus. Seth quickly seized his brother's throne, but when Horus grew older, he claimed that the throne belonged to him. Countless myths detail the subsequent conflicts between the two.

In one such myth, Horus went before a council of the gods to see what they thought. Both Seth and Horus were asked to speak for themselves. Seth declared that only he was strong enough to defend the boat of the sun as it crossed the skies. Some agreed with him, but most did not. Seth then refused to go on with the trial.

After much trickery and deceit, Seth challenged Horus to a trial of strength. He proposed that each change himself into a hippopotamus and stay underwater for three months. Horus agreed, but his mother, Isis, afraid for his safety, made a copper harpoon and threw it into the water. At first she hit Horus by mistake. Then she harpooned Seth, who begged for mercy. Isis eventually took pity on him and let him go. This so angered Horus that he cut off his mother's head. His rashness called for punishment by the gods, and Seth tore out Horus's eyes while he slept. However, the goddess Hathor restored the eyes with the milk of a gazelle.

Eventually, after Horus had appealed for justice again, the gods wrote to the dead Osiris in the Underworld to see what should be done. He threatened to send demons into the realm of the gods if justice was not forthcoming, so the gods finally agreed that Horus should be king. Seth had to accept the judgment, and Isis rejoiced to see her son crowned at last. The sun god then summoned Seth to live with him and become the god of storms.

The White Walls

The great king, Menes, stood proudly before the enemy troops and accepted their surrender. His soldiers from the southern Nile Valley, or Upper Egypt, had defeated the army from the northern Delta region of Lower Egypt. Now the whole of the Nile Valley would be one kingdom.

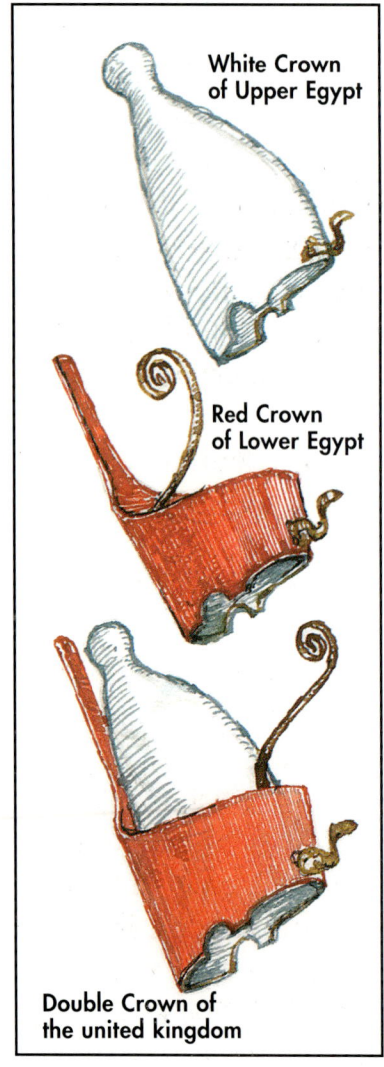

White Crown of Upper Egypt

Red Crown of Lower Egypt

Double Crown of the united kingdom

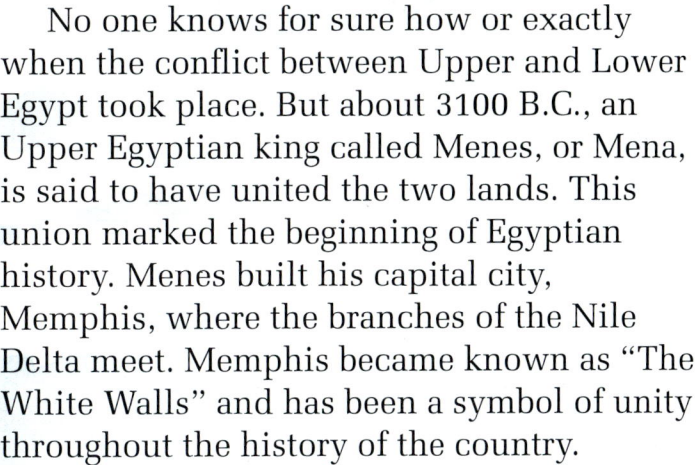

No one knows for sure how or exactly when the conflict between Upper and Lower Egypt took place. But about 3100 B.C., an Upper Egyptian king called Menes, or Mena, is said to have united the two lands. This union marked the beginning of Egyptian history. Menes built his capital city, Memphis, where the branches of the Nile Delta meet. Memphis became known as "The White Walls" and has been a symbol of unity throughout the history of the country.

In legend, Menes was the first king of the human race! But that is only legend. Probably, though, Menes did found the first dynasty of Egyptian kings. Only much later would the Egyptian king be called *pharaoh*, a name that means *Great House*. Historians call the period of the first two dynasties of kings—about 400 years—the Archaic Period. And it was during this time that Egypt was transformed from a tribal society to a state with a centralised government.

Archaeologists have used different sources to develop a picture of Egypt's earliest history. One source is the picture writing found on objects that have survived from that time. One such object is a palette called the "Narmer" palette. It commemorates a king who lived at the time of the unification. One side shows Narmer wearing the White Crown of the south, while the other shows him with the Red Crown of the north. Narmer's mace, or staff of office, shows him sitting on a throne protected by the vulture god Nekhbet. Some historians think that Narmer was the real name of the legendary Menes. Others think that Menes may have been the son of Narmer.

King Scorpion

The Egyptian peasant, or *fellah,* watched the muddy water as it gurgled along the new irrigation ditch. Then he joined the other fellahin in a cheer to thank King Scorpion for providing such a wonderful irrigation system.

Irrigation allowed the waters of the Nile River to be directed farther inland by way of irrigation ditches, or channels dug into the ground. This meant that more as well as better crops could be grown.

Archaeologists have found evidence to prove that irrigation existed in Egypt around the time of the unification. The evidence comes from part of a mace head found at the ancient Egyptian city of Hierakonpolis. It depicts an Egyptian king—whom we now call Scorpion after the scorpion sign on the mace head—opening dykes to begin the flooding of an irrigation ditch.

King Scorpion is depicted on the mace head in full ritual dress. In front of the king's face is a scorpion with a seven-petalled flower above it. This hieroglyphic probably signifies his name. Because Scorpion wears just a white crown, he is probably king of Upper Egypt only, so the scene may have taken place before unification. However, there may have been a picture on the missing side of the mace head showing Scorpion with the red crown of Lower Egypt as well.

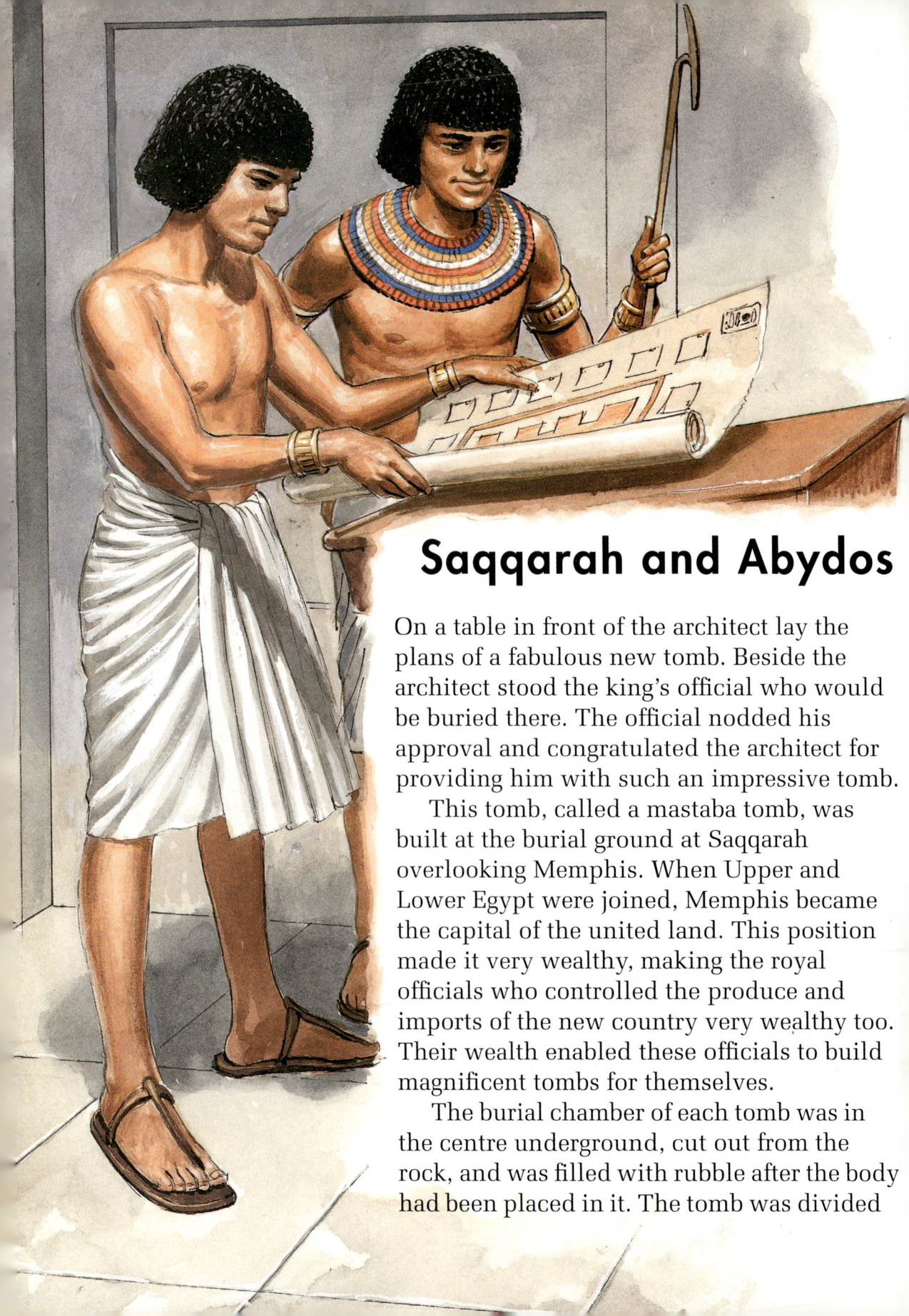

Saqqarah and Abydos

On a table in front of the architect lay the plans of a fabulous new tomb. Beside the architect stood the king's official who would be buried there. The official nodded his approval and congratulated the architect for providing him with such an impressive tomb.

This tomb, called a mastaba tomb, was built at the burial ground at Saqqarah overlooking Memphis. When Upper and Lower Egypt were joined, Memphis became the capital of the united land. This position made it very wealthy, making the royal officials who controlled the produce and imports of the new country very wealthy too. Their wealth enabled these officials to build magnificent tombs for themselves.

The burial chamber of each tomb was in the centre underground, cut out from the rock, and was filled with rubble after the body had been placed in it. The tomb was divided into different chambers, or rooms, to hold all the goods that the dead official would need in the afterlife. When all the preparations for the dead were finished, the entire complex was roofed over, leaving no entrance.

Unfortunately, the roof was often an easy way for thieves to enter the tomb, so almost all the mastabas at Saqqarah were eventually robbed of their goods.

Abydos, a town that lay 97 kilometres north of modern Luxor, was another sacred place. It is the official burial site of the god Osiris, and may have been the burial place of the early Egyptian kings. However, some Egyptologists believe that only monuments to the kings were placed at Abydos and that Saqqarah is the actual burial site.

This is a plan of a mastaba tomb.

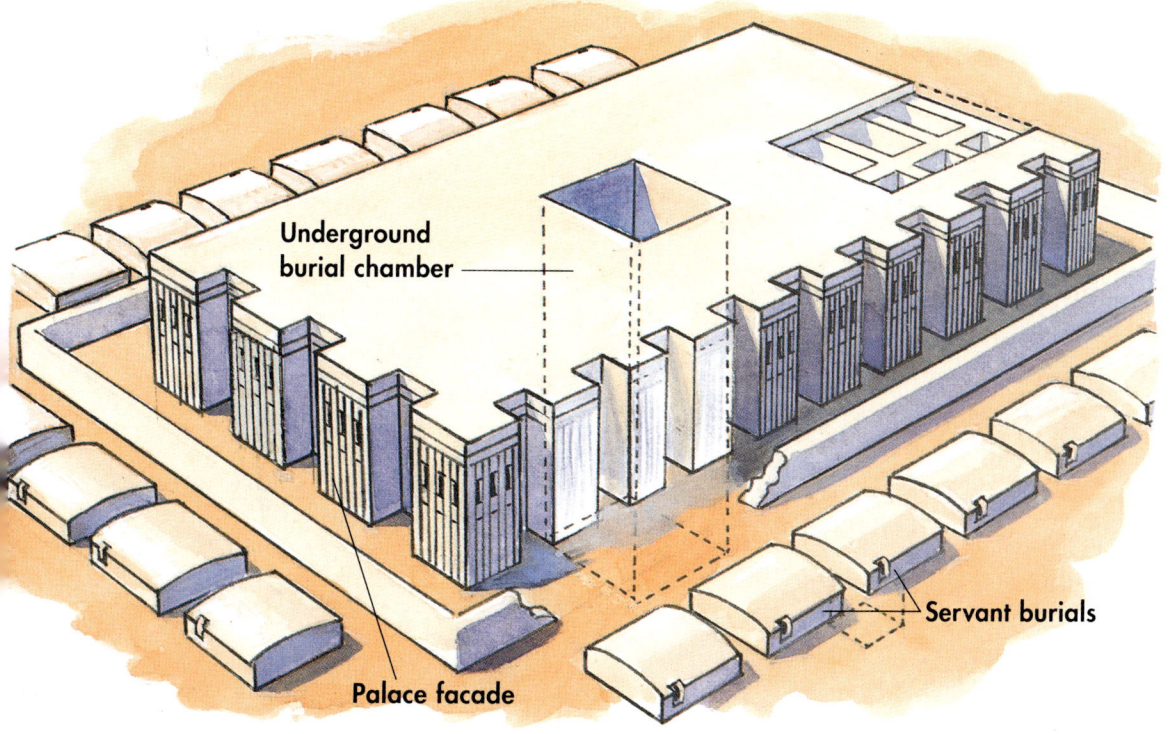

Dynasties—
the Old Kingdom

Old Manetho looked down at the document he had just completed. It was another page in his history of Egypt. Soon he would be finished with his work, and a proper record of Egypt's story would exist.

Manetho was a high priest who lived during the reigns of Ptolemy I and Ptolemy II, from 323 to 245 B.C. He wrote one of the first chronologies, or historical accounts, of the kings of Egypt. He divided Egyptian history into 30 ruling houses called dynasties, dating from the unification of Egypt in 3100 B.C. to the death of the last native Egyptian pharaoh, Nectanebo II, in 343 B.C. (though sometimes two more dynasties are added after this period).

Dynasties and Kingdoms*

*Dates are approximate.

Early Dynastic Period 3100-2686 B.C.	Old Kingdom 2686-2181 B.C.	First Intermediate Period 2181-1991 B.C.	Middle Kingdom 1991-1786 B.C.	Second Intermediate Period 1786-1554 B.C.
Dynasty I Dynasty II	Dynasty III Dynasty IV Dynasty V Dynasty VI Dynasty VII Dynasty VIII	Dynasty IX Dynasty X Dynasty XI	Dynasty XII	Dynasty XIII Dynasty XIV Dynasty XV Dynasty XVI Dynasty XVII

New Kingdom 1554-1070 B.C.	Third Intermediate Period 1070-664 B.C.	Late Period 664-343 B.C.	Ptolemaic Period 343-30 B.C.	Roman and Byzantine Period 30 B.C.-A.D. 642
Dynasty XVIII Dynasty XIX Dynasty XX	Dynasty XXI Dynasty XXII Dynasty XXIII Dynasty XXIV Dynasty XXV	Dynasty XXVI Dynasty XXVII Dynasty XXVIII Dynasty XXIX Dynasty XXX		

This is a list of the kingdoms and dynasties of Egypt.

No full text of Manetho's work still exists. But ancient scholars often used parts of it in their own histories, and Manetho's account has survived in fragments within these later works.

Manetho used many different sources to construct his history. Being a priest, he probably had access to the temple records. He also had access to official papyrus histories, the sacred books of the temples, and historical inscriptions on the temple walls. To these he added many popular traditions.

More recently, scholars have grouped the dynasties into three kingdoms—the Old, Middle, and New. Between and after these kingdoms are three Intermediate periods during which Egypt was weak and sometimes ruled by foreign kings.

The Old Kingdom began with Dynasty III, in 2686 B.C. and lasted until 2181 B.C. It included great kings such as Zoser. This was the time in which the pyramids were built.

The Pyramids

The waters of the great Nile had risen higher and higher, flooding the land along the valley. It was the time of the Inundation, and the fellahin, or peasants, could not work in the fields yet. But there was still plenty to do. Too much, thought Tinep, a fellah, as he tugged and pulled at a huge stone. It was his job, along with many other fellahin, to haul the stone up to where work was taking place on King Khufu's tomb. Tinep had been working since sunrise and was already tired. But the king must have his pyramid so that he could be properly sent off into the afterlife.

During the Old Kingdom, Egyptian civilisation developed quickly. Its power increased through centralised government; technology improved; hieroglyphic writing advanced; art progressed. Nothing else, however, compares with the great architectural feats that we know as the pyramids.

The first pyramid builder was Zoser, a king of Dynasty III. He was also called Netjerkhet, because in addition to a birth name kings were given a Horus or Seth name, depending on whether they came from the north or the south. Netjerkhet was Zoser's Horus name.

Zoser decided to build his tomb about a mile from the escarpment at Saqqarah so that it would stand out from the other mastaba tombs. The work was carried out by Zoser's vizier, Imhotep. Imhotep was a genius and was probably only second in importance to the king. The step pyramid he designed consists of six steps rising to 62 metres. Inside is a maze of shafts and tunnels.

More than 2 million separate blocks of stone were used to build the Great Pyramid. Each averaged about 2.5 short tons (2.3 metric tons).

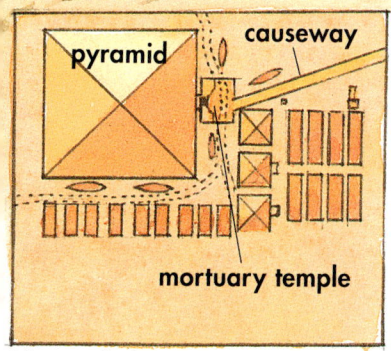
Plan of the step pyramid

The first true pyramid was built by the Dynasty IV king, Sneferu. But the greatest pyramid was built by Sneferu's son, Khufu, or Cheops. This monument originally stood about 147 metres high on the Giza plateau near Cairo. It is referred to appropriately as the "Great" pyramid, and was one of the Seven Wonders of the Ancient World.

This picture shows the gods representing the world. Nut, the sky goddess, is separated from Geb, the earth god.

The children of Amon

In the beginning there was only Amon, who came before the earth, the sky, humans, or gods existed. He lived in splendour in the watery wastes of Nun, which was chaos. Then Amon decided to create the world. From himself he created the bringer of light, Re, the sun god. After that, he created Nut, the goddess of the sky, and Geb, the god of the earth. Geb, the earth, and Nut, the sky, had four children. They were Osiris, Isis, Seth, and Nephthys. These and other gods inhabited the earth before humans.

That is how the world began according to one version of the ancient Egyptian creation myth. The ancient Egyptians worshipped many gods. The chief deity was Re, the sun god. The Egyptians relied on Re along with Rennutet for good harvests. Isis was the most important goddess, representing motherhood and the devoted wife. Her husband, Osiris—

who was also her brother—ruled over vegetation and the kingdom of the dead. The son of Osiris and Isis, called Horus, was often depicted as the god of the sky.

Each Egyptian city worshipped its own special group of gods. There were usually three—a god, a goddess, and their son. The people of Memphis, for instance, worshipped Ptah, the protector of craftsmen; Sekhmet; and their son, Nefertum.

Most ancient Egyptians prayed to their gods at home, not at temples. Each temple was the home of a particular god, and a priest was its caretaker. Priests offered prayers to the god upon people's request.

Osiris, Anubis, Horus

Life after death

The servant felt very sad as he took his place in the funeral procession. He had been fond of his master, a nobleman of Memphis, who was about to be buried. The servant thought about the small models of servants that would be placed in his master's tomb. They were used as substitutes for the real thing, and were supposed to help the dead nobleman in the afterlife. The servant hoped they would serve as well as he himself had during his master's long and happy life. Other small models were to be placed in the tomb as well,

to make the master's afterlife as comfortable as possible.

The ancient Egyptians believed strongly in life after death. They made elaborate preparations to ensure that the spirit of the dead would be comfortable. They believed that when a child was created on the potter's wheel of the god, Khnum, a double was made as well. This double resembled the body in every way and so had all the body's needs and desires. The double, called the *ka,* was stored in the heart. After death, the ka was separated from the body but remained in the tomb so as to be close to the body in which it had spent its life. It still needed all the things the body had needed in life, so food, drink, clothing, perfume, and perhaps even a servant ka, were placed in the tomb for its use.

In addition to a ka, each person had a *ba.* The ba was the soul of the person. It entered the body at birth, together with the breath of life, and left it at death.

The ka and the ba were united after death and together became an entity called the *akh.* The akh was able to inhabit the afterlife along with the gods and live for eternity. Many spells and rites were performed at a funeral to make sure that the dead person became an akh. For if the deceased did not, he or she would have to endure the horror of a second death, from which there was no return!

Two other parts of a dead person had to survive: the shadow, and the name. A person's name was his spirit of individuality. It was preserved on the tomb walls, the coffin, and equipment in the tomb. To have your name destroyed was a terrible fate.

The Mummy

The embalmers had spent the last 15 days wrapping the body of the nobleman in linen. Fingers and toes had been bound individually, then legs and torso. The head of the great man had been finished with special care to show off his features, and jewels placed between wrappings secured with resin. Now a beautifully painted mask, made of papyrus and resin, was lifted up and placed over the mummy's head. Finally the mummy was ready to be placed in its finely decorated coffin. The body was now ready for the afterlife.

The ancient Egyptians believed that the body of a person had to be preserved if his spirit was to live happily in the afterlife. So they developed a way of artificially preserving the body called mummification. The process was so lengthy and costly that only kings and the wealthy could afford it.

Mummification began with cleansing the body. Then all the internal organs were removed and preserved. Next, the body was dried in a bed of natron salts, a process that took 40 days, and anointed with perfumes and oils. The mummy was now ready for wrapping. Yards of linen strips were used for the process, which could take up to 15 days. The whole body was finally covered with a

The jars that held the organs of the person to be mummified had stoppers representing the four sons of Horus.

The Egyptians mummified cats, dogs, and even crocodiles.

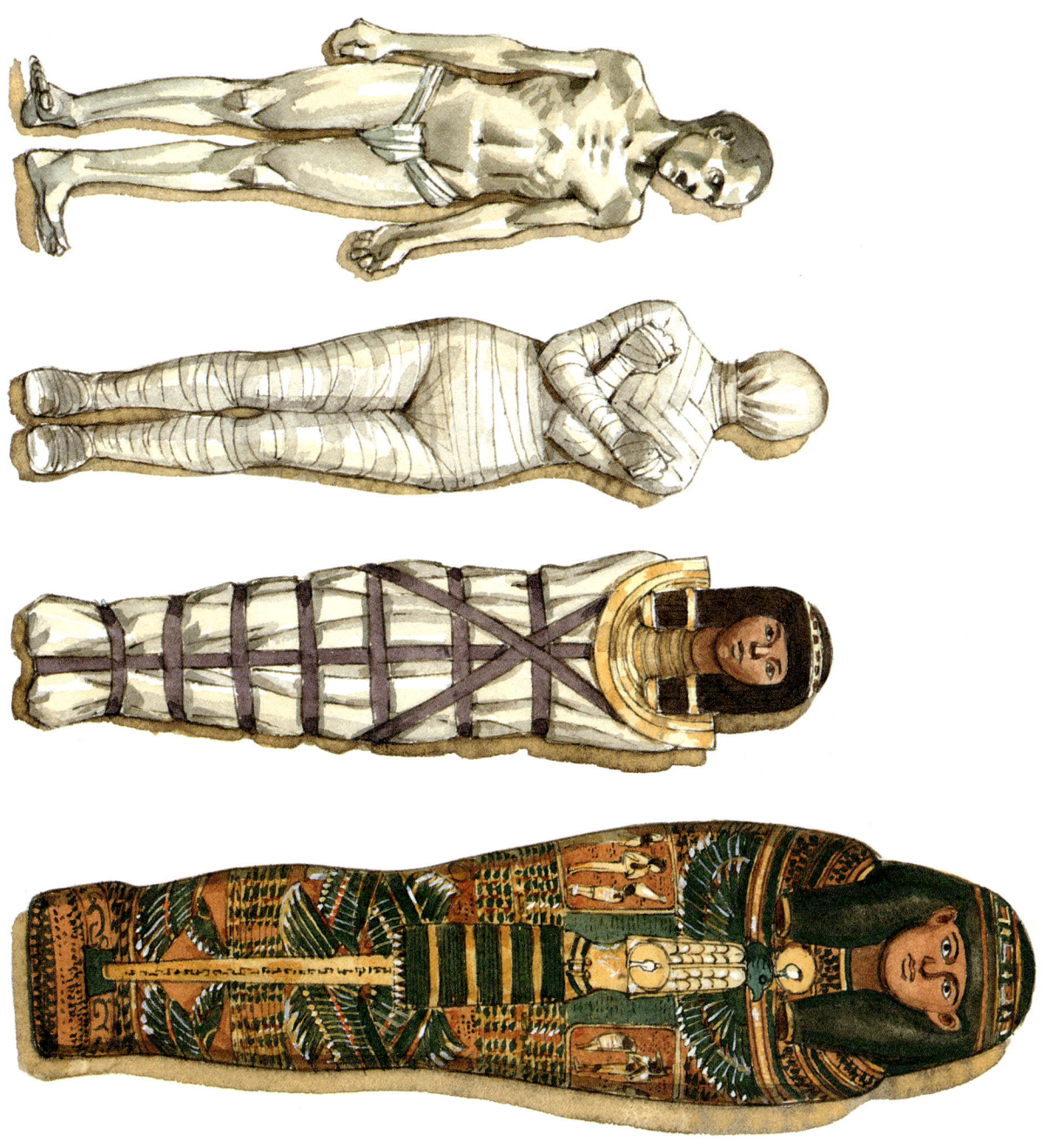

shroud held in place by more strips of linen. From the Middle Kingdom onward, a painted mask was placed on the mummy when it was ready to be put into the coffin. The whole process took 70 days.

The preparation of the mummy was done in these stages.

The Middle Kingdom

The battle had raged all afternoon under the hot sun. Now Mentuhotep I looked with pride as his pikemen charged into the last block of Nubian archers. Those who were not killed were taken as slaves by the fierce Egyptians. The victory illustrated the new power of Egypt over its enemies. Now it was time to exert that power over those Egyptian governors who had become too arrogant for their own good. These nomarchs, as they were called, had set up petty governments in their provinces, or *nomes*. Mentuhotep insisted on one government only—his own!

The last ruler of the Old Kingdom, Pepy II, held power for a long time, perhaps 94 years. During his reign, the power of the king declined and provincial governors began to take control. This shift in power was followed by a series of low Niles, when the river did not rise as usual, and Egypt fell into chaos. For about 140 years, the country was divided and at war. This time is called the First Intermediate Period. Mentuhotep I was a southern king from Thebes (modern Luxor) who managed to unite the country again. His reign marks the beginning of the period called the Middle Kingdom.

The first years of Mentuhotep's reign were ones of bitter fighting. In fact, archaeologist Herbert Winlock found a tomb at Thebes containing the bodies of 60 soldiers slain in battle. In the fourteenth year of the king's reign, he overthrew the people of Abydos in Lower Egypt and eventually extended his rule over the entire country.

Mentuhotep reigned for 50 years and guided Egypt to a new era of peace and prosperity. He indulged in building grand-scale works, the greatest of which was his temple tomb built on the west bank at Thebes. A number of Mentuhotep's close officials were buried near this tomb.

The Middle Kingdom lasted for just 250 years, and was marked by the rule of the kings of Dynasty XII. During this time, trade was built up with eastern Asia and the south, and the defensive "Walls of the Prince" were built to keep out marauding hordes from Asia who tried to infiltrate the Delta from the east.

The soldiers of Mentuhotep easily overcame their Nubian enemies.

The Hyksos

Fire raged along the streets, devouring the buildings and temples of the great city of Memphis. The townspeople ran for their lives, seeking shelter where they could. The Hyksos rode through the devastation on their chariots, cutting down soldiers and civilians. At the same time, their expert bowmen loosed arrows at any target that moved, and seldom missed. It was a terrible time for northern Egypt, under the rule of the foreigner Hyksos.

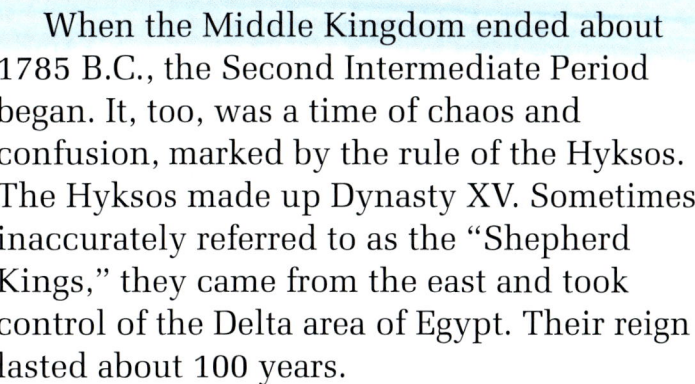

When the Middle Kingdom ended about 1785 B.C., the Second Intermediate Period began. It, too, was a time of chaos and confusion, marked by the rule of the Hyksos. The Hyksos made up Dynasty XV. Sometimes inaccurately referred to as the "Shepherd Kings," they came from the east and took control of the Delta area of Egypt. Their reign lasted about 100 years.

The Hyksos sacked the Egyptian capital of Memphis in about 1720 B.C., but did not make it their own. Instead, they operated from Avaris and Tell el-Yahudiyeh. Their main god was Seth, the god of the desert wasteland. They also brought with them from their homeland of Palestine the worship of foreign gods and goddesses. The most important were Astarte, the mother-goddess, and Reshep, the god of war and storms.

Historians do not know much about the Hyksos rulers, probably because their power was concentrated in the Delta and because Hyksos memorials may later have been destroyed by the Egyptians. One thing of value the Hyksos did leave, however, was the horse and chariot, which later Egyptian rulers put to good use in their conquests.

The Hyksos were eventually expelled from Egypt by two Theban rulers, Kamose and Ahmose. Kamose took the Hyksos capital of Avaris. His younger brother Ahmose drove the Hyksos out of Egypt and even pursued them into Palestine, laying siege to their town of Sharuhen. With the princely line of Thebes in control of Egypt, Dynasty XVIII was born and the New Kingdom began.

The New Kingdom

The soldiers on the shore of the Nile lifted their spears and shouted with glee. For down the mighty river glided the king's barge, and hanging upside-down on the prow of the vessel was the leader of the Nubian forces. Ahmose, the admiral of King Thutmose I, would never tire of telling how his enemy was hanged head downward. He was proud of the successes the Egyptians had enjoyed during the Nubian campaign, and wanted to show it.

After the Hyksos had been driven out of Egypt, the first kings of Dynasty XVIII concentrated on strengthening their borders—a task that meant bringing Nubia, which they called Kush, and Syria under control. Once this was accomplished, the brilliant New Kingdom began to flourish. It lasted from 1554 B.C. to about 1070 B.C., a period of nearly 500 years.

The pharaohs of the New Kingdom were treated as gods on earth, and in some ways they seemed godlike. They built huge temples and fortresses that can still be seen in Egypt today. We are even able to look upon the faces of some of the great New Kingdom rulers, as many of their mummies were buried in two secret hiding places that were found only in the last century. Kings such as Thutmose III, who could be considered the "Napoleon" of the pharaohs; Ramses II, who was a great builder and soldier; and Ramses III, who successfully fought off the mysterious Sea People, were all New Kingdom rulers. Other famous names include Akhenaton, the king who worshipped just one god; Queen Hatshepsut; and, most famous of all, the boy king Tutankhamen, who was found virtually intact in his tomb.

The mighty pharaohs, their buildings, and the culture they enjoyed makes the New Kingdom period one of the most fascinating in Egyptian history. We have learned more about ancient Egypt from monuments and records created at this time than from earlier times. The end of the kingdom, sometimes referred to as the Empire, marked the end of the fabulous civilisation of ancient Egypt. It would be many years before the country would prosper again.

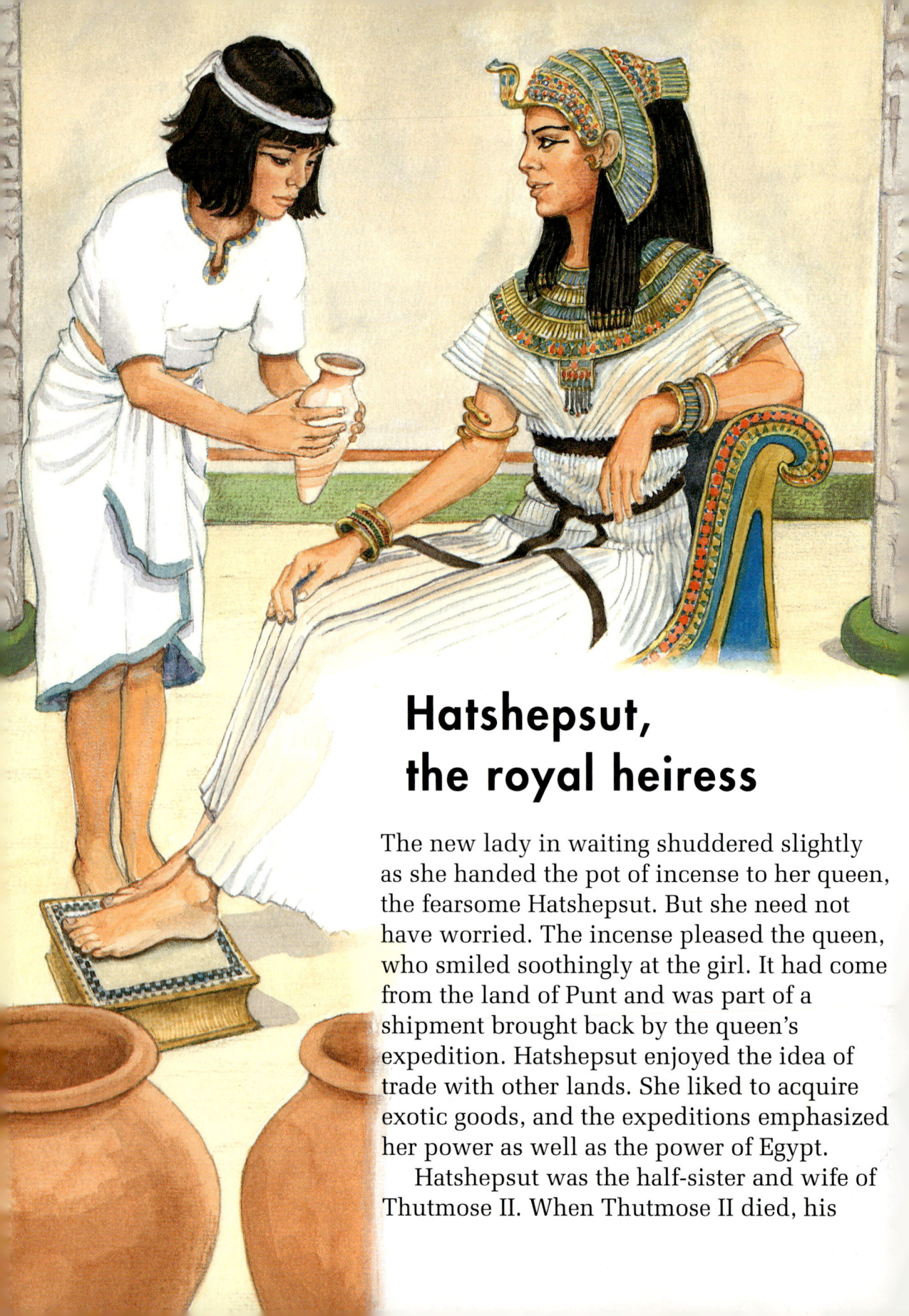

Hatshepsut, the royal heiress

The new lady in waiting shuddered slightly as she handed the pot of incense to her queen, the fearsome Hatshepsut. But she need not have worried. The incense pleased the queen, who smiled soothingly at the girl. It had come from the land of Punt and was part of a shipment brought back by the queen's expedition. Hatshepsut enjoyed the idea of trade with other lands. She liked to acquire exotic goods, and the expeditions emphasized her power as well as the power of Egypt.

Hatshepsut was the half-sister and wife of Thutmose II. When Thutmose II died, his young son Thutmose III became pharaoh, but Hatshepsut took control of the country as regent. She eventually claimed that she had been chosen by the god Amon to be pharaoh. Then she had a magnificent temple built in her own honour. In effect, she ruled Egypt for years.

Hatshepsut enjoyed the life of queen and pharaoh. She sent ships on trading missions to bring back exotic goods. In her private quarters, the queen would have had scent bottles, decorated combs, looking glasses, makeup pots, hairpins, and ointment jars. Her waiting ladies would have dressed her in long, sheathlike garments made of fine cotton that fell to her ankles, and she would probably have worn a dark wig. Around her neck would hang a beautifully wrought "collar" of precious stones.

Hatshepsut loved art and helped bring about an artistic renaissance. During her reign, Egyptian works became more lively than they had traditionally been. Her artists and sculptors decorated the many temples she commissioned; cats were a favourite artistic subject. Hatshepsut also may have listened to music. Harps, lutes, and other stringed instruments were used to accompany voices.

When Hatshepsut died, her name as king and her image were erased from every monument in the kingdom. Perhaps it was her claim to be king—and not just queen—that was too disturbing to the Egyptians' concept of the divine pharaoh. But Hatshepsut's unique temple remains as a testament to her reign.

This is the magnificent mortuary temple of Hatshepsut.

This is a sphinx statue of Hatshepsut. It was unusual for a lion-maned sphinx to have the face of a woman.

Yuya, father to pharaoh

It was a time of great famine in Canaan, and the sons of Jacob had travelled for a second time to Egypt to buy grain. When they arrived they were greeted by the same man who had provided them with grain on their first visit. They knew him only as the vizier of the great pharaoh, Amenhotep III. But to their surprise, the vizier now told them who he really was. His name was Joseph. He was their brother, the one they had cast in a pit, who was found by some passersby who sold him into slavery in Egypt so many years before. But Joseph was not angry with his brothers. He had risen in power and position in the land of the pharaohs and now was second in importance only to Amenhotep himself. In fact, he was more than that. Joseph told his brothers, "So then, it was not you who sent me hither, but God: and He hath made me a father to the pharaoh!"

The story of the sons of Jacob is a familiar one to people who have read the Christian Bible or the Muslim Koran. In the traditional story, Joseph rises in rank to become virtual ruler of Egypt and calls for his family, the tribe of Israel, to follow him there. Joseph later dies in Egypt after predicting the exodus of Moses and asking that his bones be taken back with the Israelites to his homeland to be reburied.

The trouble with this story is that the events are not recorded in Egyptian history. No one called Joseph existed. But what if his name was recorded as Yuya instead of Joseph? And what if Yuya's bones had not been taken back to Israel with Moses, but had been buried in the Valley of the Kings? Then the Biblical story would tie in with Egyptian history!

The mummies of Yuya and his wife were found in the Valley in 1904 and now rest in the Cairo Museum. We know that Yuya was the king's vizier. We also know that he had a daughter, Tiye, who married Amenhotep III. This would certainly have made him "father to the pharaoh."

However, the Bible says that the Israelites were in Egypt for 430 years. That means Joseph would have arrived much earlier than the reigns of Thutmose IV and Amenhotep III, the kings Yuya served. But Old Testament dates are often inaccurate.

Could Yuya have been Joseph? This is impossible. Yuya's mummy cannot possibly be Joseph's, because the remains of prophets are deemed to be sacred and cannot, conceivably, be exhibited to the people.

Akhenaton and the one god

The procession of chariots halted in front of the Great Temple of Aton. The chariots carrying the king, Akhenaton, his queen, Nefertiti, and their daughters, were richly decorated in blue and red with golden spheres of the sun. The horses that pulled them were also finely robed. It was time for the pharaoh to worship the god Aton. This was the only god he worshipped and the driving force in his life. Everything existed, he believed, through the goodness of Aton and Aton alone.

When Amenhotep IV took over the throne, he began a period of religious and cultural revolution in Egypt. He shunned the old god Amon and his priests, and began the cult of the sun disk, the Aton. He declared that Aton was the one god except for Re, whom he believed was part of the sunlight that came from the Aton. He also said that he was the only one who could speak with Aton, so there was no need for priests. He even changed his name to Akhenaton, which means "servant of the Aton." Finally, he banned the worship of Amon and closed down that god's sacred temples.

In his sixth year of office Akhenaton, with his wife, the beautiful Nefertiti, moved out of the capital city of Thebes to a new capital in Middle Egypt named Akhetaton—"The Horizon of Aton"—which is modern Amarna. Akhenaton's religious reforms, which historians now call the Amarna Revolution,

This is a famous bust of Nefertiti, the wife of Akhenaton.

led to an outpouring of art and sculpture that glorified the Aton. However, the new religion was probably followed only by the nobles and close followers of the king. The rest of the people may have gone on worshipping as they had always done.

Akhenaton was probably more of a philosopher than previous pharaohs, who had been interested in war and conquest. Also, Akhenaton tended to leave the governing of the country to others as he pursued his religious interests. When he died, his religious changes died with him, and Egypt returned to its traditional gods and priests.

The Boy King

Howard Carter, the British Egyptologist, had almost given up hope of ever finding anything when his workers dug away the earth under a broken-down hut. Before them was a flight of descending steps. At the bottom was a sealed door, and on it was the symbol marking a royal burial. Carter quickly replaced the rubble in front of the door and waited until his backer for the expedition could join him. Then, on the 26th of November, 1922, Carter broke down the sealed door. Behind it was a passage and a second door. And behind that door was an astounding sight: a room filled with statues, vases, chariots, inlaid boxes, and hundreds of other objects—all of them gold. It was the tomb of Tutankhamen, a king of Dynasty XVIII, who had died about 1350 B.C.

At the end of the entrance corridor was a room called the *antechamber,* and off the far left corner of that was another smaller room called the *annex.* To the right of the antechamber was a blocked door, and beyond it, the burial chamber of the king. There stood four gold-covered, wooden shrines covering a huge red quartzite sarcophagus. Inside lay three coffins, one inside the other. The last was fashioned of pure gold and held the gem-studded mummy of the dead king, its face covered by a magnificent funeral mask. Another room held the young king's treasure.

After years of archaeological work, the wonders of Tutankhamen's tomb were removed, and most were placed in the Cairo Museum. Today they are often displayed at museums around the world.

Tutankhamen's gold coffin

Tutankhamen's gold funeral mask

A picture from the painted burial chamber showing Tutankhamen being welcomed by the goddess Nut.

Little was known of Tutankhamen before the discovery of his tomb. He was probably a son of Akhenaton. His birth name was Tutankhaton, but the ending was changed to "amen" when the old religion was brought back, and Amon was worshipped as the most important god.

Tutankhamen was doubtless a "puppet" ruler with little real power. During his reign, the country was probably run by advisers to the king. He was pharaoh for about ten years when he died from a blow that fractured his skull.

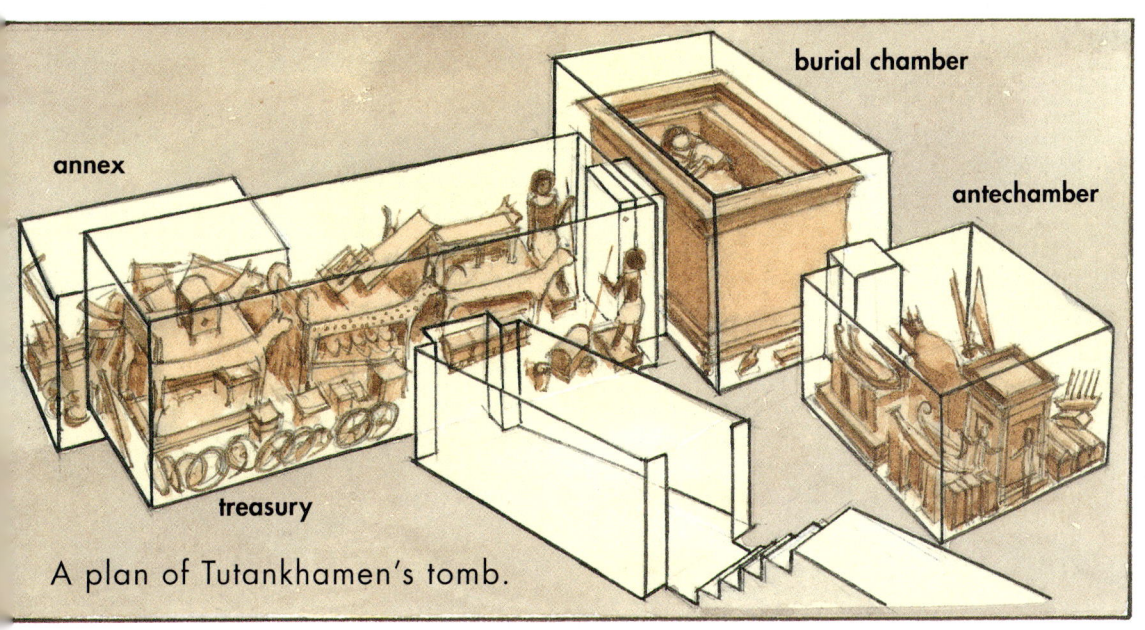

A plan of Tutankhamen's tomb.

Home life

The children giggled as they splashed around the wading pool in old Emhotep's garden. The adults sitting around the courtyard chatted or just watched the children play. The boys wore short white kilts or nothing at all, and except for one braided lock of hair, each was bald. The girls looked pretty in their ankle-length sheath dresses and shining black hair, worn long at the back with a fringe at the front. Their white clothing kept them cool in the hot sun.

   Emhotep was their grandfather. He was a high official at the court of the pharaoh and possessed a fine estate with a big house built of mud brick and painted white. It had over 30 rooms. Emhotep loved flowers and kept his courtyard full of blooms all year round. He also enjoyed pets. Several cats roamed the grounds, and two dogs lounged in the shade of a large bush. One of his grandchildren, called Kiya, stroked a large ginger cat, which purred with delight.

Emhotep had many servants and slaves. Some worked in his fields, tending the goats and cattle or growing crops, while others ran the large house. Female servants looked after the needs of his wife, who was very fond of her makeup. She wore red lip powder and outlined her eyes with green paint. Of course, in his younger days, Emhotep had used just as much makeup as she, as was the custom. Emhotep's daughter, Senamun, was very beautiful. She wore a long, white linen gown with a wide collar encrusted with jewels. On her head was a black wig, held in place with a band of blue stone. Her husband, wearing a robe over his short kilt, sat by her on a brightly painted chair on the verandah.

Soon it would be time to eat, and Emhotep had provided a particularly sumptuous feast for his family and guests. There would be antelope and gazelle meat with plenty of vegetables, including onions, garlic, lettuce, and celery. Loaves of bread would be served, and there would be beer to drink. At the end of the meal, fresh fruit would be presented, as well as cakes sweetened with honey.

When evening came, the servants would light the flax wicks of the stone lamps, and there would be music. Some of the adults would play a board game called *senet,* while others discussed the gossip of the palace. The children, though, would retire to the roof of the great house, the coolest place to sleep, and dream of another wonderful day splashing in the pool.

Time and the stars

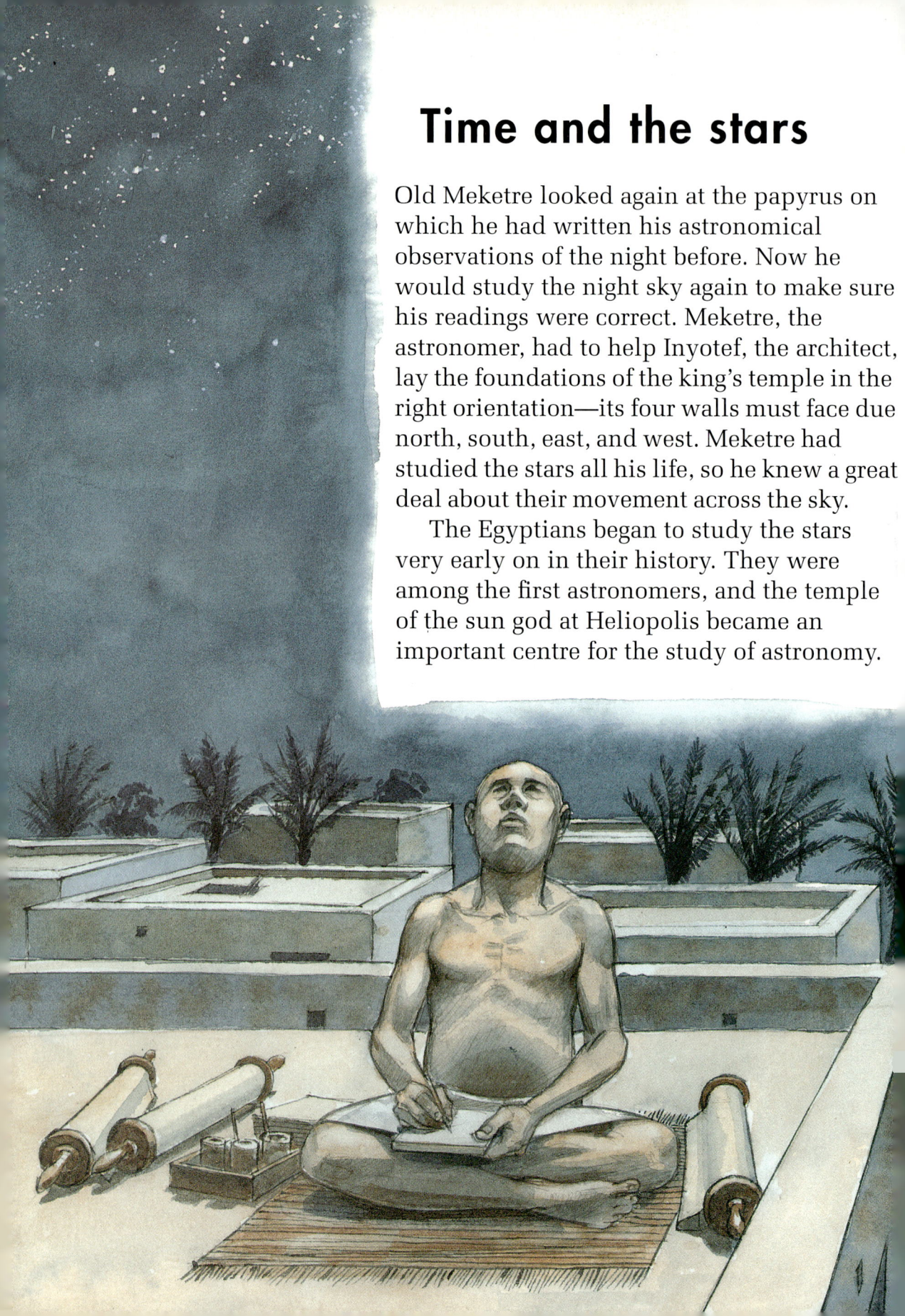

Old Meketre looked again at the papyrus on which he had written his astronomical observations of the night before. Now he would study the night sky again to make sure his readings were correct. Meketre, the astronomer, had to help Inyotef, the architect, lay the foundations of the king's temple in the right orientation—its four walls must face due north, south, east, and west. Meketre had studied the stars all his life, so he knew a great deal about their movement across the sky.

The Egyptians began to study the stars very early on in their history. They were among the first astronomers, and the temple of the sun god at Heliopolis became an important centre for the study of astronomy.

Ceiling relief of the zodiac of Dendera

For the ancient Egyptians, astronomy was closely connected with the telling of time. They observed that the rising of the dog star with the sun every year coincided with the beginning of the annual flood. This and other observations helped them develop a calendar of 365 days a year. They also divided the day and night into 24 hours, although the length of the hours changed according to the season, and were among the first people to begin the day at midnight. The Roman leader, Julius Caesar, introduced the Julian calendar, which divided the year into 365 days with a leap year every fourth year, based on contacts with Egyptian astronomers and observations they had carried out in Egypt. This calendar was used until a slightly modified version, called the Gregorian calendar, took its place in 1582. So we can thank the old Egyptian stargazers for the device we hang on our walls today!

Ramses the Great

The leather of the reins cut into the flesh of Ramses II as he pulled yet another arrow from his quiver and made ready to fire. Ramses fired and hit another of the Hittite enemy. His chariot continued to charge at breakneck speed as he prepared to fire again, and a smile crossed his face as he saw the enemy hesitate. Soon they were completely thrown into confusion by the superior Egyptian forces, and their citadel was ripe for attack. Ramses's soldiers hurriedly erected scaling ladders and began to climb. Defenders plunged from the battlements as they tried to resist. But it was useless. The Egyptians under their mighty king, Ramses the Great, were far too strong a force. Dharpur was doomed!

There are many accounts of the pharaoh Ramses II doing battle with the Hittites on Egypt's Syrian frontier. The Egyptian accounts tell of the king's bravery and his prowess as a soldier. The Hittite wars resulted in stalemate and a signed peace treaty between the two nations. However, the pharaoh is always depicted as the victor and worthy of the name Ramses the Great.

As a boy, Ramses participated with his father, Seti I, in the wars against the Hittites. He also learned from his father how to govern successfully. Even his interest in building seemed to grow at an early age, as he is often depicted overseeing the cutting of obelisks for his father's building projects.

The first part of Ramses's reign saw constant war with the Hittites. But when the leaders of both nations realised that there could be no outright winner, a peace was proposed. The peace treaty survives and can be seen today, carved on the walls at Karnak. Much of Ramses's greatness, though, comes from the incredible building works he completed, examples of which can be found all over Egypt and beyond. He added on to the great temples at Karnak and Luxor, finished his father's mortuary temple at Thebes, and built a temple at Abydos dedicated to Osiris. However, the greatest of Ramses's works are probably the two great temples carved out of the mountainside at Abu Simbel, in Nubia. The larger of the two is fronted by four colossal figures of the king that stand 18 metres high.

When Ramses died at the age of 92, he was buried in the Valley of the Kings near Thebes.

The colossal statues at the temple in Abu Simbel.

On the river

The children on the bank of the river stared in awe as the nobleman's barge drew closer. It was a fabulous sight. It even smelled wonderful, as delicate perfumes from the royal passengers wafted toward the shore. The children heard the laughter of the ladies and gentlemen and the gentle swish of the oars as they broke through the water. The noble party sat in an open cabin at the centre of the boat. They dined from tables piled high with fruit and sweetmeats, and drank dark red wine from silver goblets. The oarsmen sat at wooden benches on either side of the cabin, and from the stern a helmsmen steered the vessel with two long, straight rudders. A pilot at the bow of the vessel held a long pole for sounding the depth of the river.

In ancient Egypt, the Nile River was the country's main highway, carrying both goods and people. The earliest riverboats were made of papyrus stalks bound together. They were very light and could be carried easily. These boats were used by fishermen in their daily work.

Later boats, especially those used for pleasure by officials and royalty and those used for trade, were made of wood. These boats carried a single mast and a large square sail. Papyrus rope was used for the rigging. The very large barges used for carrying obelisks of granite were towed along by other, smaller vessels because they were too unwieldy to operate under their own power.

Pitch was used to make a papyrus boat waterproof.

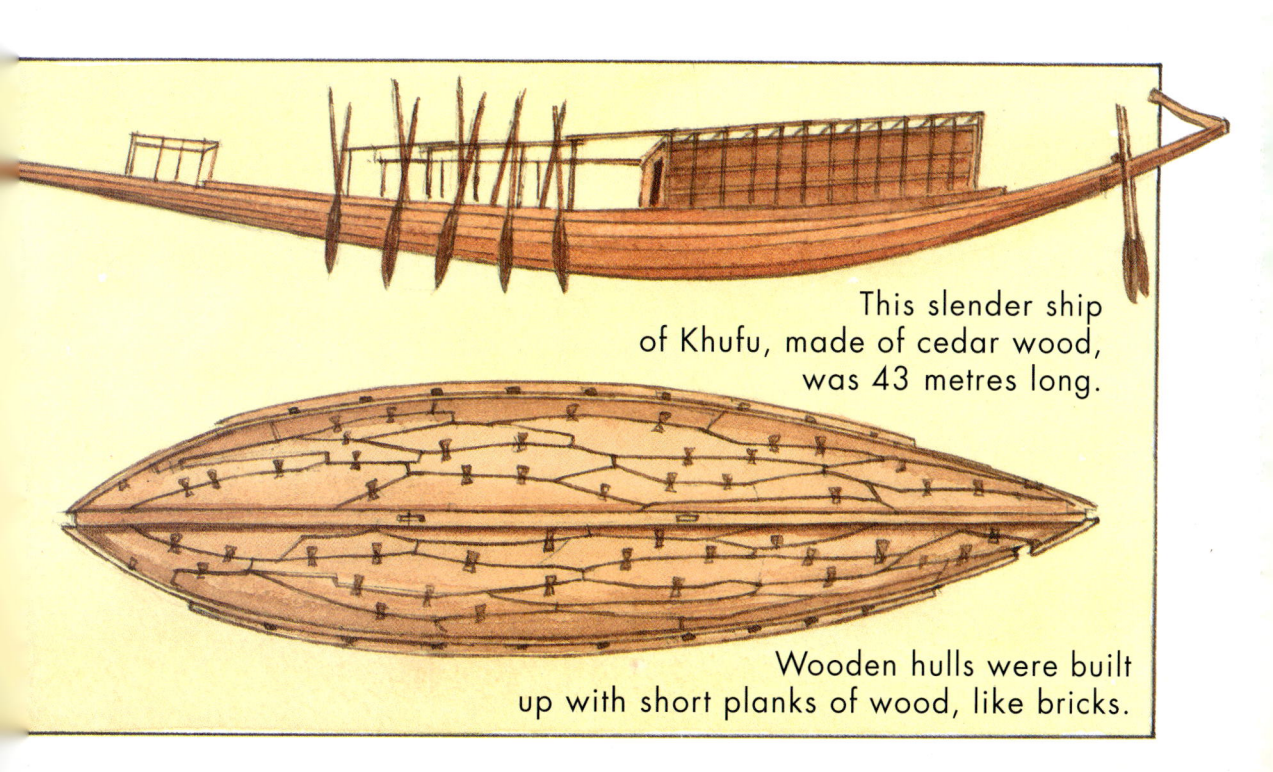

This slender ship of Khufu, made of cedar wood, was 43 metres long.

Wooden hulls were built up with short planks of wood, like bricks.

The Sea People

Ramses III had defeated the armies of the Sea People on land; now he must destroy their fleet of ships standing offshore near the Nile Delta. The pharaoh raised his hand and gave the call to fire. The ranks of archers lining the shore let loose with their arrows, pouring volley after volley into the enemy ships. At the same time, "marine archers" standing on the decks of Egyptian ships fired from close range. When enemy ships came close enough, they were hauled alongside with grappling hooks and their crews killed. Ramses's army was triumphant again, and the Sea People were vanquished once and for all.

During the reign of Ramses III, the peoples of the Middle East were in turmoil. Desperately looking for land on which to settle, they fought amongst themselves and against the mighty Hittites of Asia, whom they defeated. Then they joined forces and looked toward the fertile valley of Egypt. The confederation that resulted included Peleshet, or Philistines; Tjeker; Shekelesh from Sicily; Weshesh; and Denyen. Together, they became known as the "Sea People."

The Sea People made their way overland via Syria, where they stopped for a time. From there they moved west, determined to force their way into Egypt and settle. In the meantime, their fleet stood off the Egyptian coast waiting to attack. Ramses III knew that he had to move quickly, so he ordered his eastern frontier posts to stand firm until he brought up the main army. The battle took place on the border. The Egyptians slaughtered their enemy with apparent ease.

Now Ramses had to face the threat from the sea. And he was as effective at destroying the Sea People on water as he was on land. Egypt was safe again. Ramses reigned for 31 years, surviving a conspiracy to murder him. He died during the trial of the conspirators, a death that ended the reign of the last great pharaoh of Egypt.

This is the cartouche of Ptolemy found on the Rosetta Stone, compared with the cartouche of Cleopatra. You can see how some letters are the same.

The Rosetta Stone

The writing on the wall

Young Pum looked dejectedly at the papyrus roll in front of him. He had been copying hieroglyphics all morning. His teacher, the ancient scribe Merenra, whom they called Hippora because he looked like a hippopotamus, was standing over him holding a fly whisk. Hippora would use the whisk on Pum if the boy even looked up from his papyrus. Still, if Pum wanted to be a scribe himself, then he had to learn to write even better than his teacher. Being a scribe led to a comfortable, well-paid job. But for now, it was just more copying!

In ancient Egypt, the education of a scribe could take up to 12 years to complete. The most important goal of this education was learning to read and write the Egyptian picture writing called hieroglyphics. The word hieroglyphics is made up of two Greek words—*hieros,* which means sacred, and *glyphe,* which means carving.

For centuries, no one could actually read Egyptian hieroglyphics. Then, in 1799, the famous Rosetta Stone was discovered at Rashid in the Western Delta. The stone is a copy of a decree issued in Memphis in 196 B.C. by priests commemorating Ptolemy IV. It is written in three scripts: Egyptian hieroglyphs, Egyptian demotic, and Greek. The Greek text was easy to read and soon the names of the Ptolemaic rulers were recognised in the demotic text. Then Thomas Young, an English scientist, discovered that the hieroglyphic script consisted of phonetic signs, and that the royal names were written in ovals called cartouches. This led to the breakthrough in deciphering hieroglyphics, achieved by the French scholar Jean-François Champollion.

We now know that hieroglyphic writing is divided into Old Egyptian, Middle Egyptian, and Late Egyptian. Hieroglyphics eventually developed into hieratic, in which the figures are joined. After 700 B.C., another form of cursive, or connected, writing was used in Egypt. This writing, called demotic, was one of the scripts found on the Rosetta Stone.

Hieroglyphic writing

Hieratic writing

Demotic writing

تعتبر الجيزة من أهم أحياء القاهرة الفخمة على الشاطئ الغربي

Modern Arabic writing

The priests

The priest watched as the mummy of the rich noble was raised to an upright position at the entrance to its tomb. Low-ranking priests purified it with water and incense, while others chanted the words of an ancient ritual. The high priest then raised an adze-like instrument to the mummy and to the Ka statue. Finally, he touched the mummy with a pesesh-kef knife and stood back. Now the senses of the body of the dead noble were restored. The Opening of the Mouth Ceremony had been successful.

This ceremony, along with many others, was conducted by the priests of ancient Egypt. Priests were ranked with the officers of the state who ran the country on behalf of the pharaoh. The head of every priesthood was the pharaoh himself, as he alone could mediate between humans and the gods. High priests during the period of the early kingdoms were probably members of the royal family and therefore very close to the pharaoh. In villages, though, the priest may have been simply the wise man of the village who looked after the local god. He may have been assisted by a number of subordinate priests. All priests had to be trained scribes.

During the New Kingdom, the priesthood became a highly specialised profession as considerable wealth was lavished upon state gods. The chief priests were now great administrators as well as religious leaders. In Thebes, for instance, four prophets, or high priests, were required as well as a host of minor priests, down to the official bearer of floral offerings. This priesthood was, in turn, supported by a whole society of workers. The priesthood was virtually a state within a state.

The most important priest was the First Prophet, or High Priest of Amon at Thebes. His temples received such lavish gifts from the grateful pharaohs that it took four senior prophets to administer the revenues. The second of these prophets, or priests, was probably a close relation to the king or his chief queen. During the reigns of the later Ramses pharaohs, the First Prophet became virtual ruler of Upper Egypt, and the title became hereditary, son following father.

A satrapy

Ephrahim's wife placed a jar of sweet-tasting seremt on a wooden stand in front of her husband. A servant helped his master drink the beverage by holding a long reed syphon that fed into the jar. Ephrahim, a spearman working as a mercenary soldier for the pharaoh of Egypt, reflected on how easy life had been lately, putting down a few minor revolts. He hoped things would not change, but there were rumblings about a Persian invasion, and that could be disastrous. The Persian Empire was strong, and its king, Cambyses, was a mighty warrior. Perhaps, thought Ephrahim, it might be time to seek a new master!

By the end of Dynasty XX, Egypt had begun a slow decline, and the country had once again divided into two. About 945 B.C., a family of Libyan descent took over the throne, beginning Dynasty XXII. Their rule ended in chaos, and the Amon-worshipping king of Kush, or Nubia, successfully invaded Egypt. The Kushites, beginning Dynasty XXV, ruled for nearly a century, until another family of Libyan descent displaced them. These Saite kings founded Dynasty XXVI, and brought stability to the country for about 100 years. But the Saites were never completely trusted by the Egyptian people, and some Egyptians rose up in revolt. This unrest weakened the country and laid it open to invasion by the Persians, who were expanding their empire.

In 525 B.C., Egypt fell into the hands of the well-organised Persians without much

resistance. Their ruler, Cambyses, governed the country as the first king of Dynasty XXVII, making it part of his vast Persian Empire. He ruled from the Persian capital of Susa and employed governors called *satraps* to run the country. They, with Egyptian collaborators, were successful for nearly two centuries. Only for a short period in the 4th century B.C. did Egypt briefly regain its independence. When Egypt fell to the Persians for a second time, in 343 B.C., the reign of Nectanebo II, the last Egyptian pharaoh, came to an end.

Alexander the Great

Alexander the Great stood in the silence of the oracle of the god Zeus-Ammon at the oasis of Siwah. Alexander was here to consult the oracle, an act the Egyptian people would look upon favourably. They had already welcomed him as a saviour, freeing them from the Persians. Now he wanted to be seen as more than just a mortal. Visiting the oracle would fulfill that wish. From now on, he would be considered the son of the god Zeus-Ammon, the new pharaoh, and king of Egypt.

After the death of his father, Philip II of Macedonia, Alexander had taken up the fight against the crumbling Persian Empire. He

A portrait of Alexander, showing him with the ram's horns of Amon.

marched southward against the Persian forces, brushing aside any opposition he encountered. In 333 B.C., after trekking through Asia Minor and the Levant, Alexander finally met the Persian King Darius III at Issus. There Alexander's forces soundly defeated the Persian army, and in 332 B.C., the victorious Macedonian troops marched into Egypt.

Alexander did not stay long in Egypt, but his influence was great. He founded the city of Alexandria at the mouth of the Nile, and restored temples that had been devastated by the Persians. Under Alexander, Egypt became part of that larger Mediterranean realm of Greek culture called the Hellenistic world.

When Alexander left Egypt, he campaigned eastward and extended his empire as far as India. It was a magnificent achievement. Unfortunately, Alexander died of illness in Babylon in 323 B.C., at just 30 years of age.

Before his death, Alexander had appointed his favourite general, Ptolemy Soter, to govern Egypt. It was Ptolemy Soter who founded the Ptolemaic Dynasty that was to rule the country for the next three hundred years.

Ptolemy

Ptolemy's men surrounded the wagon that held the large, coffin-like box. They motioned for the driver to step aside and for the guards not to interfere. Quickly they pulled the box down from the wagon and carried it to their own nearby. Then they set off for Egypt with their prize. The captain smiled to himself. He and his men had stolen the body of Alexander the Great.

With Alexander's death, his huge empire began to break up quickly. Ptolemy, who had been Alexander's boyhood friend, acted as the satrap of Egypt for Alexander's two immediate successors—Philip, his brother, and Alexander IV, his son. But both were murdered, and Ptolemy ruled as virtual king, answerable only to Perdiccas, Alexander's regent. However, Ptolemy wanted complete control of the country. So, to gain a political and religious advantage, he ordered the taking of Alexander's body. The body was being carried to Macedonia for burial. But at Damascus, it was seized by Ptolemy's men, who said that Alexander had really wanted to be buried at Siwah in Egypt. In fact, the body was first taken to Memphis, then buried at a tomb in Alexandria.

Perdiccas was furious and he immediately marched against Ptolemy. But he was defeated at Memphis and eventually murdered by his own men. The generals of Alexander continued to fight among themselves for power, and Ptolemy allied himself with two of the strongest. The allegiance worked. When the turmoil ended, Ptolemy had added Palestine and Lower Syria to the Egyptian empire he controlled.

However, Ptolemy still had to forge a link with the old line of pharaohs, so he married the daughter of Nectanebo II. Now he was king indeed, and he began the usual pharaonic ritual of building temples, towns, and monuments. The best known of them was the Pharos, or lighthouse, of Alexandria, which became one of the Seven Wonders of the Ancient World.

Hellenistic Egypt

The young scholar from Thebes looked around the large room shelved with books and marvelled at how much knowledge must be contained within it. Today was his first day in Alexandria, and this was his first encounter with the greatest library on earth.

The great library at Alexandria was just one of the wonders to be found in Egypt during the time known as the Hellenistic period. *Hellenistic* means *Greek;* at this time Egypt, along with much of the Mediterranean and Middle Eastern world, was under the influence of the Greeks. It even had pharaohs of Greek origin—the Ptolemies. The Ptolemies built up the Egyptian navy. They allowed themselves to be worshipped as gods by their subjects, thereby continuing the traditional Egyptian concept of the divine king. Also in keeping with Egyptian ways, they built huge temples and monuments.

But perhaps most important, the Ptolemies introduced into Egypt the Hellenistic love of learning and enquiry. They founded the library at Alexandria, making Egypt one of the most important centres of learning in the ancient world. The library formed part of the research unit that is known as the Museum, or Alexandrian Museum. It was located in the palace grounds. The organisation of the library was carried out by Demetrius Phalerus, who was familiar with the library at Athens.

Most of the works kept in the library were written in Greek, although there may have been translations into Greek from other languages. The librarians at Alexandria produced a body of work by the Greek poets, divided works into "books" as we now know them, and introduced a system of punctuation. They also compiled a national biography, which became a standard Greek text before it was lost.

The library and museum survived for many centuries, but they were both destroyed in the A.D. 200's during a civil war.

Cleopatra, last of the Ptolemies

Julius Caesar, ruler of all the Roman Empire, knew that he was in the presence of someone special. Before him, in all her glory, sat the Egyptian queen, Cleopatra. This woman would make Egypt great again if she were allowed to. Caesar bowed his head toward her, little knowing just how important Cleopatra would become to him.

After much family squabbling and several murders, the throne of Egypt fell to the 17-year-old daughter of Ptolemy XII—Cleopatra VII. Cleopatra was given the throne on the proviso that she marry her brother, Ptolemy XIII. She complied, but it was not long before he and his courtiers tried to dispose of her.

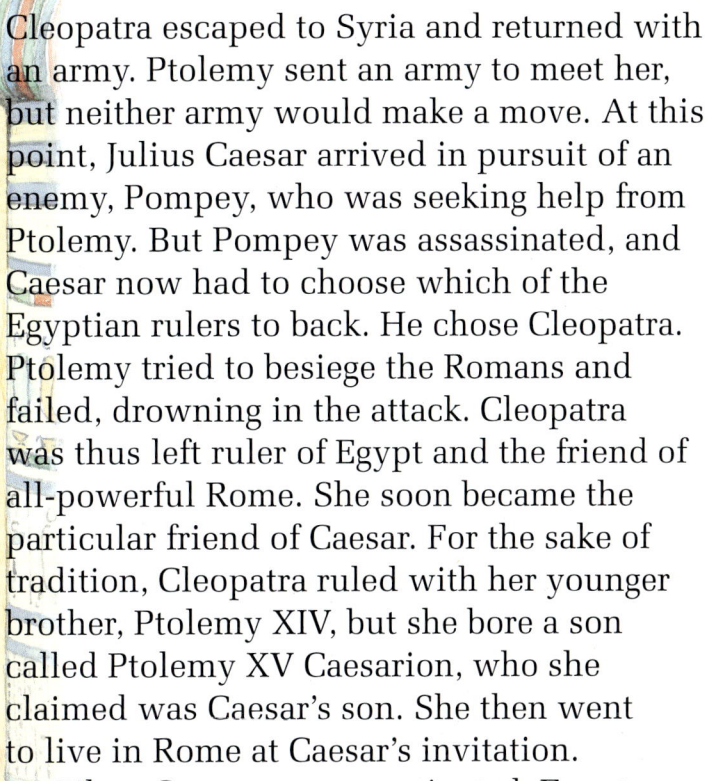

Cleopatra escaped to Syria and returned with an army. Ptolemy sent an army to meet her, but neither army would make a move. At this point, Julius Caesar arrived in pursuit of an enemy, Pompey, who was seeking help from Ptolemy. But Pompey was assassinated, and Caesar now had to choose which of the Egyptian rulers to back. He chose Cleopatra. Ptolemy tried to besiege the Romans and failed, drowning in the attack. Cleopatra was thus left ruler of Egypt and the friend of all-powerful Rome. She soon became the particular friend of Caesar. For the sake of tradition, Cleopatra ruled with her younger brother, Ptolemy XIV, but she bore a son called Ptolemy XV Caesarion, who she claimed was Caesar's son. She then went to live in Rome at Caesar's invitation.

When Caesar was assassinated, Egypt became a pawn amid the struggle for power between Caesar's heir, Octavian, and Mark Antony. Cleopatra sided with Mark Antony, with whom she had fallen in love. The struggle came to a head at the sea battle of Actium on the west coast of Greece. The battle swung from one side to the other, until for some unknown reason Mark Antony broke away from the fight and followed Cleopatra's ships into the open sea. Octavian pursued them to Egypt the next year and entered Alexandria in triumph. Rather than be humiliated by Octavian, Cleopatra committed suicide by clasping a poisonous snake to her breast. Mark Antony had earlier killed himself by falling on his sword. Octavian had them buried together at Alexandria.

The Granary of Rome

The field glowed like a carpet of gold under the harsh sun. It was not gold that caused the field to glow, though, but ripe wheat. In truth, the grain was worth almost as much as gold to the Egyptians, who sold it to the Romans. In the field, men cut the wheat with sickles. The crop was then carried to the threshing floors by donkeys, where it was trodden by oxen. Women then winnowed the wheat, and the grain they produced was taken to granaries, where it would be stored. Once a year, it would be taken to Rome. Egyptian grain was very important to the Romans, who needed it to make bread. So Egypt became no less than the granary of the Roman Empire.

When Cleopatra and Mark Antony died, Egypt was annexed by Rome. It became the personal estate of the Emperor Octavian (who later became Augustus), rather than just another province. It was ruled by a prefect who was answerable only to the emperor.

Roman emperors after Augustus styled themselves pharaohs just to maintain the appearance of being legitimate Egyptian kings. But in fact they were Roman rulers and only played at observing the traditional ideals and religion. The true Egypt of the pharaohs had vanished with the last native pharaoh, Nectanebo II, in 343 B.C.

This relief at Dendera shows the Roman emperor Trajan as the pharaoh making an offering to Hathor.

Roman Egypt

Gaius looked around him as the steam rose from the water of the hot bath. He might have been in Rome, judging by the building around him. But he was not. He was in exotic Egypt. Gaius wanted to visit the pyramids and other Egyptian monuments, but he was glad to have his baths and his villa. After all, Egypt was a

A Roman villa

prosperous part of the Roman Empire and should look the part. Gaius would enjoy his bath, then go and attend the prefect, who governed Egypt for its Roman rulers.

Egypt had indeed become a wealthy province, and many new cities had been founded. Especially in the Fayum area, one could visit classical Roman bathhouses, wander through the marketplaces, and tour basilicas. Not many monuments from the Roman Period still stand in Egypt, but some do. One of the best-known buildings from Roman Egypt is called Pharaoh's Bed, or Trajan's Kiosk. It was built on the island of Philae by Trajan, a Roman ruler from A.D. 98 to 117, and was supposed to be a grand entranceway to the Temple of Isis. But it was never finished.

Egypt continued to be the "granary of Rome" and to enjoy its wealth until the end of the second century. Then, during the reign of Commodus, from A.D. 180 to 192, Egyptian supplies had to be supplemented from North Africa. At the same time, the coins used in Egypt dropped in value. Later, the Roman Empire was divided into east and west. The Emperor Diocletian stopped administering Egypt as a separate province and made it part of the eastern empire. Egypt was split into three provinces: the Thebaid, Aegyptus Jovia, and Aegyptus Herculia. About A.D. 341, a new province named Augustus was formed, and later Herculia was renamed Arcadia. There was now a civil administrator as well as a military one. Egypt also used the same coins that were in use generally in the empire. Things would remain much this way for several centuries.

The Christians

In the marketplace, a crowd had gathered. Before the people stood a man, a foreigner. He was probably a traveller from Judah or some other northern place. Quietly the man raised his hands in the air, and the crowd stopped talking and shuffling about. When the crowd became silent, he began to talk. He told them about a man called Jesus of Nazareth, who had come to earth as the son of God. He told them about miracles and about the sad death of Jesus. Then he explained how Jesus had risen from the dead and gone to heaven. He said that he was now a follower of Jesus and his teachings, and that there were many others like him. They were called Christians, and his name was Mark.

According to tradition, the Christian church in Egypt was founded by St Mark. His teaching and the teaching of others converted many native Egyptians to Christianity. At the time, native Egyptians were known as Copts. Their main language, Coptic, was the final stage of ancient Egyptian and had an alphabet made up mainly of Greek letters with some Egyptian demotic. It became, and remains, the language of the Christian church in Egypt, which is called the Coptic Church.

In A.D. 330, the Emperor Constantine turned away from Rome and set up his capital at Byzantium, which he rebuilt and renamed Constantinople. After years of Christian persecution by the Romans, Constantine recognised the Christian church and established freedom of worship throughout the Roman Empire.

A dramatic change occurred, however, in A.D. 451, when the Coptic Church held firm to a doctrine that there was only a single nature in Christ—part human and part divine—rather than two natures as defined by the orthodox church. This led the Coptic Church to break away from the main church and to become independent. The Coptic Church remained so until the coming of Islam.

The rise of Islam

To the east of Egypt, across the Red Sea, lies the land called the Arabian Peninsula. In the 6th century, the main cities of the peninsula were Makkah and Yathrib (now called Medina). Makkah was prosperous, and the Quraysh tribe was its aristocracy. The Quraysh were the guardians of the pagan religion that was prominent in the city.

In A.D. 571, a boy called Muhammad was born into one of the Quraysh families. He became an orphan while he was still very young and was sent to the desert to live until he was 6. After that, he was raised by his grandfather and then by an uncle and was educated for a career in commerce. Despite his work, Muhammad lived a mystical and solemn life. He spent long hours meditating in a cave at Mount Hira'a. One day, as he meditated, he saw the angel Gabriel, who was commanded by Allah to recite some verses. Gripped with astonishment, Muhammad, Peace and Prayers be upon Him, then recited the verses, which told of an all-powerful and omnipotent god. He then fell into a trance and when he awoke, he believed he was the Prophet of Allah and had been chosen to spread Allah's Message to the world.

Muhammad soon had a small following in Makkah. He preached of the one God, of the evils of idolatry, and of the coming of the final judgement day. However, he could not influence the Quraysh, who finally drove him out of Makkah. In 622, he and his followers headed to Yathrib (Al Madinah Al Munawarra).

At Yathrib, Muhammad, Peace and Prayers be upon Him, became a venerated leader, both political and religious. The new faith was called Islam: i.e., obedience and submission to the Lord of the Worlds. He called on all people to become Muslim: to obey and submit to Allah. Through this faith, all Muslims became brothers, loving and helping one another.

When the Prophet and his followers went to war against the idolaters it was only to restore the dignity of the Muslims who, tormented by the people of Makkah, were forced to migrate to Al Madinah. By 631, many inhabitants of the city had converted to Islam in sufficient numbers to secure the seizure of Makkah. And when the Prophet, Peace and Prayers be upon Him, took Makkah, he gained control over most of the people of the Arabian Peninsula.

Muhammad, Peace and Prayers be upon Him, and his followers entered the sacred harram. They broke all the idols around the Ka'aba. However, the Ka'aba, that sacred abode (shrine), was not harmed in any way. It was the holy place of worship of the Muslims.

Two years after entering Makkah, Muhammad, Peace and Prayers be upon Him, died. All the verses of the Quran were collected in one volume, during the time of the Caliph Abu Bakr. It was called Muss'haf and it comprised all the divine provisions that were inspired to the Prophet of Allah, Peace and Prayers be upon Him, for all the people.

The invasion

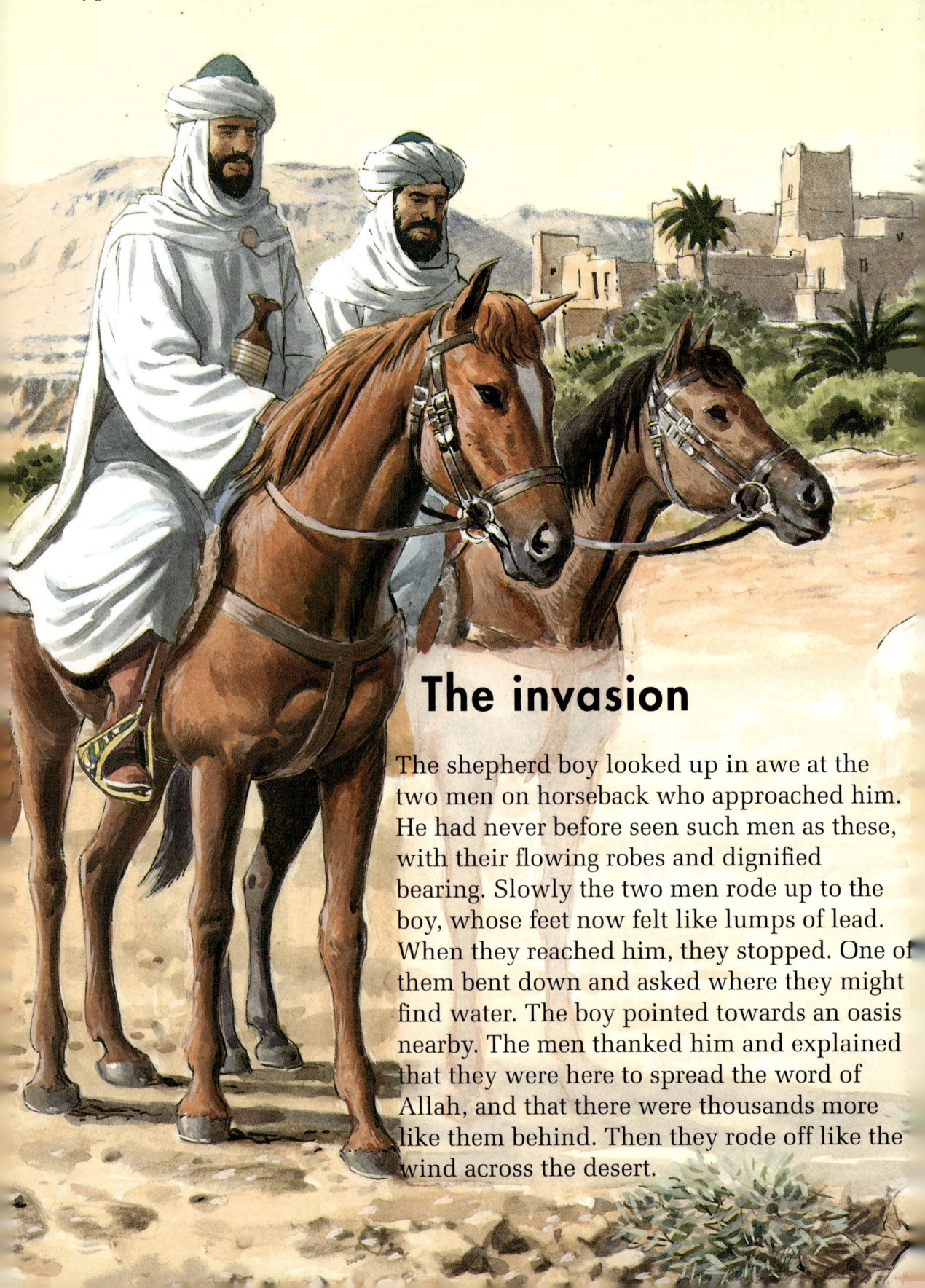

The shepherd boy looked up in awe at the two men on horseback who approached him. He had never before seen such men as these, with their flowing robes and dignified bearing. Slowly the two men rode up to the boy, whose feet now felt like lumps of lead. When they reached him, they stopped. One of them bent down and asked where they might find water. The boy pointed towards an oasis nearby. The men thanked him and explained that they were here to spread the word of Allah, and that there were thousands more like them behind. Then they rode off like the wind across the desert.

When the prophet Muhammad, Peace and Prayers be upon Him, died, his followers quickly pushed out of Arabia and into the lands nearby—first Iraq, then Syria, Palestine, and finally Egypt. The Muslim armies might have been smaller than those of the Persians or Byzantines, but they were far more mobile, and their soldiers fought passionately for Islam.

The Muslims were highly tolerant with peoples embracing other religions, and many of those people, whose lands were invaded by the Muslims, became convinced of Islam.

The Muslim invasion of Egypt came in December of 639. An Arabian general named Amr ibn el-As, with 4,000 cavalry, rode across the Sinai Desert, advanced through Pelusium and Bilbeis and attacked the fort of Babylon. It took six months to capture. Amr made his headquarters at Fustat, a new town in what is now Old Cairo, which became afterwards the capital of Egypt in place of Alexandria.

Like other countries that were part of the Byzantine Empire, Egypt was unhappy with the way it was ruled. This uneasy situation made it simpler for the Islamic army to overrun Egypt, because the Egyptians felt little affection for—or loyalty to—their Byzantine lords. And once under Muslim rule, most Egyptians in time converted to Islam.

The Fatimids

Ahmed walked with his brothers and father to the Al-Azhar mosque, where they would pray. Afterwards, he would study the Koran, and then do some mathematics.

Ahmed was a Shiite Muslim. He believed, like all Shiites, that the caliph, or Islamic ruler, must be someone directly descended from the prophet Muhammad. His own caliph was a direct descendant of Muhammad's daughter, Fatima, so the caliph and his ruling dynasty were known as Fatimids.

The Fatimids had come from Syria in 909 to what is now Tunisia. Their aim was to conquer Baghdad, the Islamic capital at the time, and there set up a new Shiite caliphate. First, though, they had to conquer Egypt.

In the beginning, Muslim Egypt was under the caliphate at Medina, then Damascus. But due to internal conflict, its power declined, and in 868 Egypt became more or less independent under its governor ibn Talun. His dynasty ended in 905, when the forces of the Abbasid caliphate in Baghdad invaded. Their governors ruled for only 30 years, however, and from 935 until 969, Egypt again enjoyed semi-independence under the Ikhshidid dynasty. The Ikhshidids had survived several attacks by the Fatimids from the west, but in 969 the Fatimids struck a final blow. They made Egypt the centre of their expanding empire and broke all ties with the Abbasid state.

The Fatimids founded the city of Al-Qahirah and made it their capital in 973. The empire of the Fatimids grew to be vast. It stretched over North Africa, Sicily, Egypt, and part of the Arabian Peninsula. Under the Fatimids, Egypt became prosperous and an illustrious centre of Islamic culture. The Fatimids also enjoyed strong military leadership. During the last two reigns, the power of the army commanders grew and they became the ruling force in the empire.

By the mid-1100s, though, the Fatimids had been weakened by fighting among various factions. And to make matters worse, they were threatened by a new danger from across the Mediterranean—the crusaders!

The crusaders

The Christian pilgrim had travelled for months to reach the Holy City of Jerusalem. He felt uplifted as he approached the sacred wall to pray. But before he could begin, two pairs of rough hands clasped his shoulders and dragged him away. The pilgrim protested loudly as the Turkish soldiers bundled him off and threw him into a prison cell, but his cries went unheard. The pilgrim was angry and confused. Christians had never been prevented from visiting the holy places in Jerusalem, even though the city was in the hands of the Muslims.

When the Arab followers of Muhammad captured the Palestinian city of Jerusalem, they acknowledged that it was sacred to both themselves and the Christians. So they allowed Christian pilgrims to visit the city and worship freely. The situation changed, however, when the Seljuk Turks—some of whom were known for their ruthlessness and who came from the plains of central Asia—took over Syria and Palestine. They refused to allow Christian pilgrims to enter Palestine, and any who did risked their lives.

Farther north, the Turks threatened Constantinople, the capital of the Christian Byzantine Empire. Its emperor appealed to Pope Urban II for help from Christians in the west. Pope Urban passionately asked the nobles and knights of Europe to go to Byzantium to enter the Holy Land usurped by the Turks.

Immediately preachers went out to the countries of Europe recruiting for what they called the Holy War. Many knights and nobles volunteered to go, and each had a large cross sewn onto his clothing. The Latin word for *cross* is *Crux,* and from this came the word *crusade*—the war of the cross. The Crusades began in 1096 and lasted for about 200 years.

The Christians wanted to create a state of their own around Jerusalem, and this they did when the Holy City was captured during the First Crusade in 1099. Then, in 1168, the crusaders attacked Egypt. The sultan of Syria sent his Kurdish commander, Shirkuh, to Egypt to help fight off the Christians. Shirkuh was made vizier, or chief minister, to the Fatimid ruler, but died soon after. However, he was succeeded by his nephew, as vizier. This man's name was Salah, better known in the West as Saladin.

Saladin

Saladin looked up at the mighty Citadel that guarded Cairo. It was a splendid fortification. Saladin, who had ousted the Fatimid rulers of Egypt and made himself sultan, hoped that it would last for hundreds of years and protect the city long after he was gone.

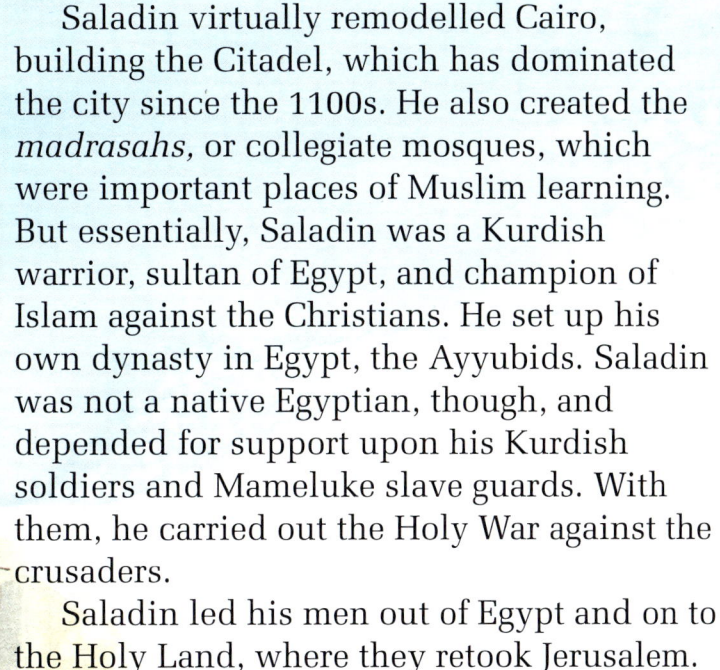

Saladin virtually remodelled Cairo, building the Citadel, which has dominated the city since the 1100s. He also created the *madrasahs,* or collegiate mosques, which were important places of Muslim learning. But essentially, Saladin was a Kurdish warrior, sultan of Egypt, and champion of Islam against the Christians. He set up his own dynasty in Egypt, the Ayyubids. Saladin was not a native Egyptian, though, and depended for support upon his Kurdish soldiers and Mameluke slave guards. With them, he carried out the Holy War against the crusaders.

Saladin led his men out of Egypt and on to the Holy Land, where they retook Jerusalem. But unlike the enemy, who had behaved disgracefully when they had captured Jerusalem, Saladin ordered his soldiers not to kill anyone in the Holy City. He also allowed Christians to buy their freedom. A wise and honourable man, Saladin was greatly admired by the Christians, and Richard the Lion-Hearted had more respect for him than for many of his allies!

Saladin died in 1193. For the next 20 years, there were more battles against the crusaders. After the failure of the Seventh Crusade, Egypt was left alone, its part in the Crusades finished.

The Ayyubid dynasty was short-lived, but it helped Egypt develop. The Ayyubids brought orthodox Sunni Islam back to the country and made Egypt a centre for Islamic learning and culture once again. They also brought the Mamelukes to the country in large numbers.

The slave kings

The slave market rang with the shouts of buyers and sellers. In one corner, above the din, a wealthy general called for a second inspection of a tall Armenian. He looked just the right sort to become a Mameluke—strong, with intelligent eyes and dignified bearing. After a few minutes of bargaining, the slave was his. Perhaps one day this slave would become the sultan of Egypt!

Strange as it may seem, the sultans of Egypt, after the fall of the Ayyubid dynasty, were once slaves. They were known as the Mamelukes, a word which means *owned,* and had first come to Egypt with Saladin and his uncle. Imported from outside the Muslim area in Europe and Asia, they were given a basic education, converted to Islam, and trained as soldiers. The relationship of the Mameluke to his master was an odd kind of slavery, though. It was one of kinship rather than servitude. So the slave often succeeded his master in a position of authority and power. And if he were strong and ruthless enough, he might even become sultan.

The Ayyubid dynasty ended with the murder of the last caliph by Mameluke troops, under their commander, Baybars. They then chose one of their own as the new ruler, the chief Mameluke, Aybak. Aybak began a period of Mameluke rule in Egypt that lasted from 1250 to 1517. There were two dynasties of Mamelukes, the Bahri Mamelukes, who ruled Egypt until 1382, and the Circassian Mamelukes. Both took their names from the barracks where their corps were quartered.

No Mameluke ruler was secure without the support of his retainers, and so more slaves were imported. They became the ruling class in Egypt and the only people to have political rights. The fellahin were considered merely providers of food and other materials.

Egypt under the Bahri Mamelukes became a major force in the Muslim world. But under the Circassian Mamelukes, Egypt's fortunes declined until constant bickering weakened the country and led to its conquest by the Ottoman Turks.

Baybars, the panther

The sultan Baybars stood by his horse at the oasis postal station. He watched as a rider galloped towards a pair of horses that stood in readiness. The rider swiftly stopped his mount, flung himself onto one of the waiting animals, and galloped off into the desert. Baybars nodded his head in approval. His postal system seemed to be working well.

The postal service was just one of the things the Mameluke sultan, Baybars, started. He also fostered public works, built beautiful mosques, and provided charitable institutions with gifts of money. He was the first Egyptian sultan to appoint four judges, representing the four religious sects. But most of all, Baybars was a military leader of great ability.

Baybars was originally a Turkish slave and worked his way up to the highest position in the land. He rose in power mainly through violence and bloodshed, but he was, after all, a trained warrior. Baybars was brave and energetic, and in addition he possessed all the charismatic charm of a born leader. He fought many campaigns against the crusaders, but his most important victory came against the Mongols in Palestine.

The Mongols were nomadic people from Asia who had swept west, looking for land, food, and plunder. In 1260, they had sacked Baghdad and were heading towards Egypt when Baybars, under the command of his Prince Qotoz, confronted them at Ayn Jalud. His army was victorious, stopping the Mongol invasion from progressing farther. Had they been successful in invading Egypt, Egyptian history would be far different from what it is today.

Baybars then proceeded to strengthen his position at home by installing as caliph in Cairo al Mustansir, a descendant of the Abbasids who had survived the sacking of Baghdad. This move made Baybars' authority more legitimate and rallied other Muslims around him. But al Mustansir was caliph in name only. The real power lay with Baybars and his Mamelukes. Baybars also strengthened his position by making wise alliances.

Baybars died in 1277 at Damascus. He is credited with being the true founder of the Mameluke dynasty in Egypt.

The Ottomans and decline

The merchant looked out at the deserted port. He wondered how long this lack of trade would go on. If business did not improve, he would be ruined. The European buyers had found a new way to the East—sailing around the tip of Africa. The merchant knew he was not alone in his troubles. Egypt was declining as a trading centre and becoming weak. Soon it would fall prey to the new menace from the East, the Ottoman Turks.

In the 13th century, under a fierce leader called Osman, or Othman, a group of Islamic

The Ottomans defeated the Mamelukes using modern weapons. The Mamelukes still felt that personal valour was most important in battle. The use of gunpowder changed all that, as it would do in the rest of the world as well.

Turkish tribes originally from central Asia took over lands east of Constantinople. By the middle of the 1400's, the Ottoman Turks, as they were called, had conquered the city. Under Osman's son Orkhan and his successors, the Ottomans brought Islam to Europe's southeastern corner. The Ottoman Empire had begun. During the next century, the Ottomans conquered the Arab world as well as Egypt and west to the Berber lands.

In Egypt, the Ottomans replaced the Mamelukes and created a decline in the country's fortunes. International traders bypassed Egypt, and the country became a mere shadow of its former glorious self.

Everyday life in Ottoman Egypt

Ali sat down beside his plough and felt a twinge of pain in his back. In the distance, he saw the dreaded tax farmer coming. Ali felt like an old man, although he was only 30. Still, he had the blessing of Allah, which comforted him. He had heard stories about the great empire of the Turks, of which his land, Egypt, was a part, and he'd once seen a Mameluke prince on his horse. But he cared little for them. The most important thing for him was Islam.

Despite the turmoil and change that had beset Egypt since the time of the pharaohs, the fellahin, or peasants, lived more or less as they had always done. Most now spoke Arabic, though, and were devout Muslims. Their religion was far more important to them than their country or its rulers. Their life, however, was hard. The fellahin had no rights. They were expected to provide the ruling classes with food and other necessities.

Under the old system, all the land had belonged to the crown and was rented out for payment of taxes. The taxes were paid in kind—that is, in goods. Now much land had been granted to soldiers and religious leaders who could decide what to do with it. The fellahin were little better than slaves in this feudal system. They cultivated the land and returned most of what they grew in taxes.

The Ottomans tried to reduce the amount of tax the fellahin had to pay. They also improved irrigation systems and brought more land under cultivation. They tried to organise a central tax system, but it soon failed. Tax collection was given over to tax farmers, who paid a certain amount to the Ottoman viceroy and kept the rest. Under the new landowning class, the fellahin had to pay higher and higher taxes. Administration was placed in the hands of officials in each village, and the fellahin were responsible to them. This made the fellahin even more isolated from the ruling classes and the cities.

The Egyptian prince

Joseph stood in awe behind the Egyptian lieutenant. At just 13 years of age, Joseph had been taken from his home in Anatolia, now Turkey, to be sold as a slave in Egypt. His master was to be a lieutenant of the Ottoman guard in Egypt. Joseph hoped he would be allowed to train as a Mameluke and one day avenge himself.

Joseph was indeed trained as a Mameluke and went on to become a lieutenant of the Mameluke beys. At 30, he was bey of the governing council of Egypt. Ali Bey, as he was now called, had enemies as well as friends. After being chosen *shayk al-balad,* or governor of Cairo, in 1763, he was forced to flee to Arabia.

Ali Bey was able to rise to his position of authority because of the governing system imposed on Egypt by the conquering Ottomans. The Ottoman sultan appointed a viceroy to represent his authority in Egypt. He also left a group of soldiers to act as the imperial military force. The chief officers of these troops served as the viceroy's council. But the sultan allowed a third group to exist—the Mamelukes, who had declared allegiance to him. So although the Mamelukes had been conquered, they still retained power in the country. These Mameluke beys became governors of the various provinces of Egypt and were known as the Egyptian princes.

Before long, the Mamelukes held the greatest power. By 1700, the viceroy was their pawn. At the same time, the Ottoman troops were absorbed into the country and lost any power they had. The Mamelukes came to control the finances and administration of Egypt. Once again, they became the true rulers of Egypt.

Ali Bey became the strongest of the Mameluke beys. In 1766, he won back his position of *shayk al-balad.* He brought 6,000 Mamelukes and 10,000 North African troops to strengthen his position and married a Russian woman. Then, when war broke out between Russia and Turkey, Ali Bey declared Egypt's independence and proposed to fight on the Russian side. He sought treaties with Russia and other states and refused to pay any more money to the Ottomans. Next, he invaded Syria. But he was betrayed by his rival Ismail Bey and killed in 1773. Ismail returned Egypt to Ottoman control, but even so, it remained in the hands of the Mamelukes.

Napoleon and Europe

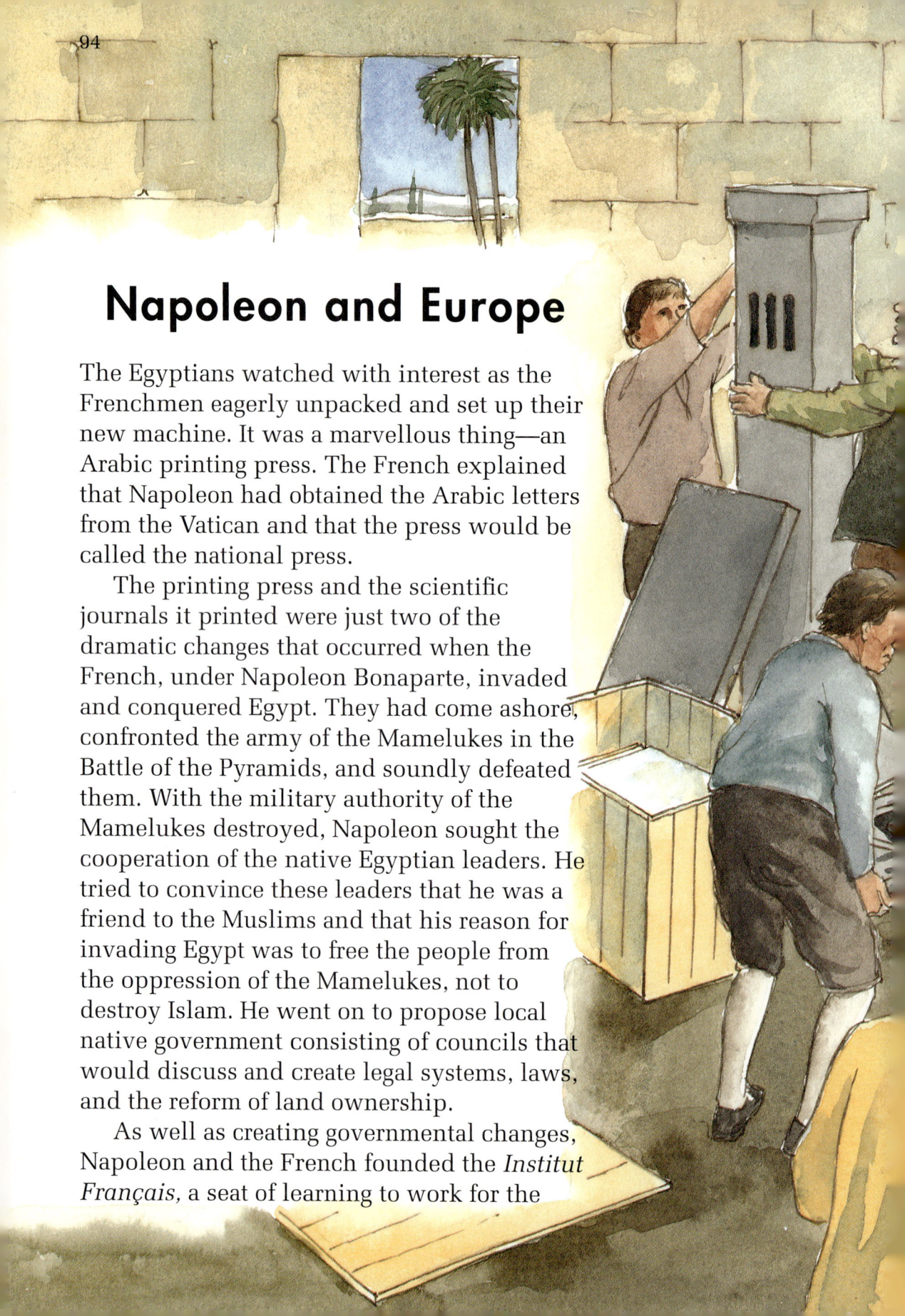

The Egyptians watched with interest as the Frenchmen eagerly unpacked and set up their new machine. It was a marvellous thing—an Arabic printing press. The French explained that Napoleon had obtained the Arabic letters from the Vatican and that the press would be called the national press.

The printing press and the scientific journals it printed were just two of the dramatic changes that occurred when the French, under Napoleon Bonaparte, invaded and conquered Egypt. They had come ashore, confronted the army of the Mamelukes in the Battle of the Pyramids, and soundly defeated them. With the military authority of the Mamelukes destroyed, Napoleon sought the cooperation of the native Egyptian leaders. He tried to convince these leaders that he was a friend to the Muslims and that his reason for invading Egypt was to free the people from the oppression of the Mamelukes, not to destroy Islam. He went on to propose local native government consisting of councils that would discuss and create legal systems, laws, and the reform of land ownership.

As well as creating governmental changes, Napoleon and the French founded the *Institut Français,* a seat of learning to work for the advancement of science, economics, the arts, literature, and other disciplines. French scientists and engineers also worked on improving roads, building factories, and constructing arsenals.

Although such actions seemed good for Egypt, Napoleon's actual purpose was the colonisation of the country for the good of the French. He also imposed harsh taxes on the people. Opposition to him was not long in coming. The Ottoman government worked against Napoleon, and the British, under Lord Nelson, destroyed French ships, cutting off the French in Egypt from France. Then open rebellion erupted, especially in Cairo in 1798. The rebellion was quickly put down. However, with Ottoman attacks and British help, the French were forced out of Egypt. The Ottomans were in charge again, but Egypt would never be quite the same.

Modern Egypt begins

The soldiers of Muhammad Ali looked scornfully at the Mameluke bey as he rode away from the estate. The bey and his family had lived off the estate for many years. But now Muhammad Ali had demanded taxes from them that they could not pay, and they had been thrown off the land.

Land confiscation was just one of the ways Muhammad Ali took control of Egypt. He had already gotten rid of most of his potential opposition—the Mameluke beys—by massacring them in Cairo. It was merciless but necessary to secure his power.

Muhammad Ali was born in Kavalla in 1769. He became leader of the Albanian mercenary soldiers in Egypt—troops of the Ottoman Empire—and then governor of Egypt. But his ambition was to make himself as powerful as he could within the Ottoman Empire. When the Ottoman sultan needed help to subdue the Wahabis in Arabia, he sent for Muhammad Ali. Ali punished the rebels, and Arabia fell under his power.

At home in Egypt, Muhammad Ali began to make profound changes. Before he took power, most of the land ostensibly belonged to the state but was, in fact, portioned out to tax farmers who owned it in all but name. They paid only a set amount of tax, and anything they collected over that was theirs. Muhammad Ali believed too much money was going to the farmers. He therefore imposed high taxes on them. When they could not pay, he removed them from the

Muhammad Ali—commander, industrialist, agriculturist, and entrepreneur.

land. Very soon, all of Egypt was back in the hands of Muhammad Ali and he distributed land as he saw fit.

Muhammad Ali's main concern, though, was to build up a strong army. He created a military school at Aswan and imported European military experts to teach there. He also established a war department and a war council. In addition, he created a European-style state school system and sent individuals to Europe to be trained.

Muhammad Ali took control of industry and trade. All of this development was basically to help Muhammad Ali maintain power, which it did. It also created an enemy out of Great Britain. In 1841, the British forced Muhammad Ali to limit the size of his armies. By the time of his death in 1849, many of his reforms were failing.

New government

Omar sat down at his desk. He was fresh from a year's hard work in France and now could speak the French language almost perfectly. He was looking forward to his job in the new Foreign Affairs department of Muhammad Ali's modern government. He felt proud to be here, especially being an Egyptian, because many of the posts were held by Europeans. But Omar had skills that many Europeans did not. He could speak six languages, including Turkish and Arabic.

The overall ruler of Egypt was the sultan of the Ottoman Empire, of which Egypt was a part. The sultan delegated power to the governor of Egypt, Muhammad Ali. But the empire was weak and could not really control what Muhammad Ali did, so in reality Muhammad Ali ruled Egypt. And unlike previous governors, he had no contenders for power. His authority, and therefore his government, was absolute and centralised. Muhammad Ali set up a government that worked efficiently from top to bottom. He divided the land into provinces. These were divided into governorates, provinces, districts, and departments, much like the divisions to be found in European countries. He then appointed governors, subgovernors, inspectors, and mayors to administer the various areas. They formed a chain of command that was ultimately responsible to Muhammad Ali.

The central government was made up of executive heads of departments, or ministers, who were responsible for the different functions of the government. They were close friends of Muhammad Ali and were loyal to him, rather than to Egypt or the system. At the same time, Muhammad Ali got rid of the Cairo council and the general council of Egypt, replacing them with a Council of State and a Private Council made up of aides rather than representatives of the people. Turkish continued to be the language of government for a time, but it was gradually replaced by Arabic. And, although Muhammad Ali stood by the sharia, or Muslim code of laws, he also began the study of French-modelled civil, criminal, and commercial law, which would later be adopted.

Muhammad Ali's government certainly created order in Egypt, and in doing so it brought in many useful systems. It helped move Egypt along the road to modernisation.

King cotton

Monsieur Louis Jumel, the French engineer and cotton expert, looked out across the new cotton crop and nodded his approval. Two Egyptian cotton dealers standing nearby were equally delighted. They watched the fellahin picking the cotton and tallied up how much profit they could make. Little did they know that this white fluffy stuff would one day be Egypt's most important cash crop.

Once Muhammad Ali had created his monopoly over agriculture and its products, he introduced into Egypt a very saleable cash crop—cotton. Before long the cotton plant

Contemporary Egyptian cotton textiles in brilliant hues

was being intensively grown along the Nile. This cultivation increased production for export, which made money for Muhammad Ali, but it also provided raw material for his textile industry. Thus, he made even more money, as well as keeping more people employed. His ownership of both the textile industry and the cotton fields provided him with huge revenues.

The cotton grown in Egypt was, and is, the long-fibred variety. It is known for its strength and durability. These qualities made it easy to sell to countries with their own textile manufacturing industries. During the U.S. Civil War, U.S. ships blockaded cotton-exporting ports in the southern United States, increasing the need for exports from Egypt. The production and export of cotton and the textile industries in Egypt have remained an important part of the country's economy, and Egyptian cotton goods are famous around the world for their quality.

Suez

The man watching nearby winced as a massive explosion sent rocks and debris flying in all directions. At the same time, the dam broke, and a wall of water tumbled into the waiting Suez Canal. Ferdinand de Lesseps, who had been in charge of digging the canal, was glad the job was over. Now there was a much more rapid way for ships to travel from Europe to the East.

By the time Muhammad Ali died, he had established his family as the ruling dynasty in Egypt. He had been succeeded by Ibrahim, Abbas I, and then Said. Said, a son of Muhammad Ali, wanted to see Egypt develop into a European-style country. Said was a kind and lenient man, but he could also be weak and was easily swayed by those around him. He became friends with the French engineer Ferdinand de Lesseps, a charming and persuasive man. De Lesseps talked Said into considering a Suez canal that would link the Mediterranean with the Red Sea, providing a quick route to the East for Europeans. Finally, Said granted the famous concession to dig the canal in 1854.

Thousands of builders were employed. In some places, solid rock had to be blasted through, while in others, mud had to be scooped up, squeezed free of water, and packed into walls. And all this work had to be carried out under the searing heat of the desert sun. Once the canal was finished, it stretched for about 190 kilometres. By 1869, cargo ships were sailing through it.

The Suez Canal created a short cut that allowed ships to sail from the Mediterranean, through the Red Sea, to the Indian Ocean, without having to go all the way around Africa. The journey to India no longer took three months. It took just three weeks! But the canal also created problems for Egypt. The British did not like the fact that it was a French operation and might hinder their imperial plans in the East. At the same time, the new ruler of Egypt, Ismail, had managed to get his country into great debt through his modernisation programme. Ismail's need for money tempted him to sell his shares to the British for 4 million pounds sterling, making the British the largest single shareholder in the canal. The British now had a hold over Egypt that would cause even more problems in the future.

Urabi and nationalism

Colonel Ahmad Pasha Urabi and his troops surrounded the home of Sultan Pasha. Inside, members of the assembly had gathered to discuss the crisis in Egypt. The khedive was in danger of being overthrown by Urabi, and help from foreign armies might be needed to stop them.

Meanwhile, the army had insisted that Urabi be reappointed as Minister of War. Urabi was determined to have his way. He threatened to depose Tawfiq Pasha, the khedive, if the members did not support him. The assembly members finally urged the khedive to restore Urabi to the War Ministry.

However, Egypt was still in chaos. It had all begun with the debts the country had built up. Egypt owed millions to various European countries, and foreign powers intervened to try to sort out the situation. The khedive Ismail had been forced to step down, and his son Tawfiq was made khedive in his place. Tawfiq was now seen as a puppet of the foreign powers. A British fleet had sailed into the harbour at Alexandria to underline Britain's intentions. Tawfiq then formed a government that included several European controllers, who were supposed to look after their countries' financial interests in Egypt and help Egypt become solvent again. But Egyptian intellectuals, landowners, and members of the army did not like this European interference. And the army had the force to do something about it.

On May 28, 1882, pressed by army officers, Khedive Tawfiq issued a decree maintaining

Ahmed Urabi as Minister of Defence, then rushed to Alexandria to be close to the British fleet. Urabi was now virtual ruler of Egypt. Tension mounted as days passed. By July, Urabi's troops were building up defences against the British fleet, which had arrived on May 20, 1882, to Alexandria's waters, increased the numbers of their men, and overwhelmed the population. The British asked Urabi to stop fortifying shore defences, but he did not. Thus, on July 11, the British fleet opened fire. Colonel Urabi declared war on Britain while the khedive, supported by the British, was barricaded in his Ras El-Tin Palace. Then British troops landed and began to engage with the British garrison. Urabi and his troops stopped resistance and the rebellion was over. Urabi was arrested.

Urabi was a simple soldier who was eventually promoted to the rank of Lieutenant Colonel. Landlords and intellectuals had seen in his rebellion against Khedive Tawfiq a chance to gain more power through having a national government and getting rid of foreign rule. And Urabi's own army colleagues had wanted to be promoted, to be paid better, and to be rid of foreign officers.

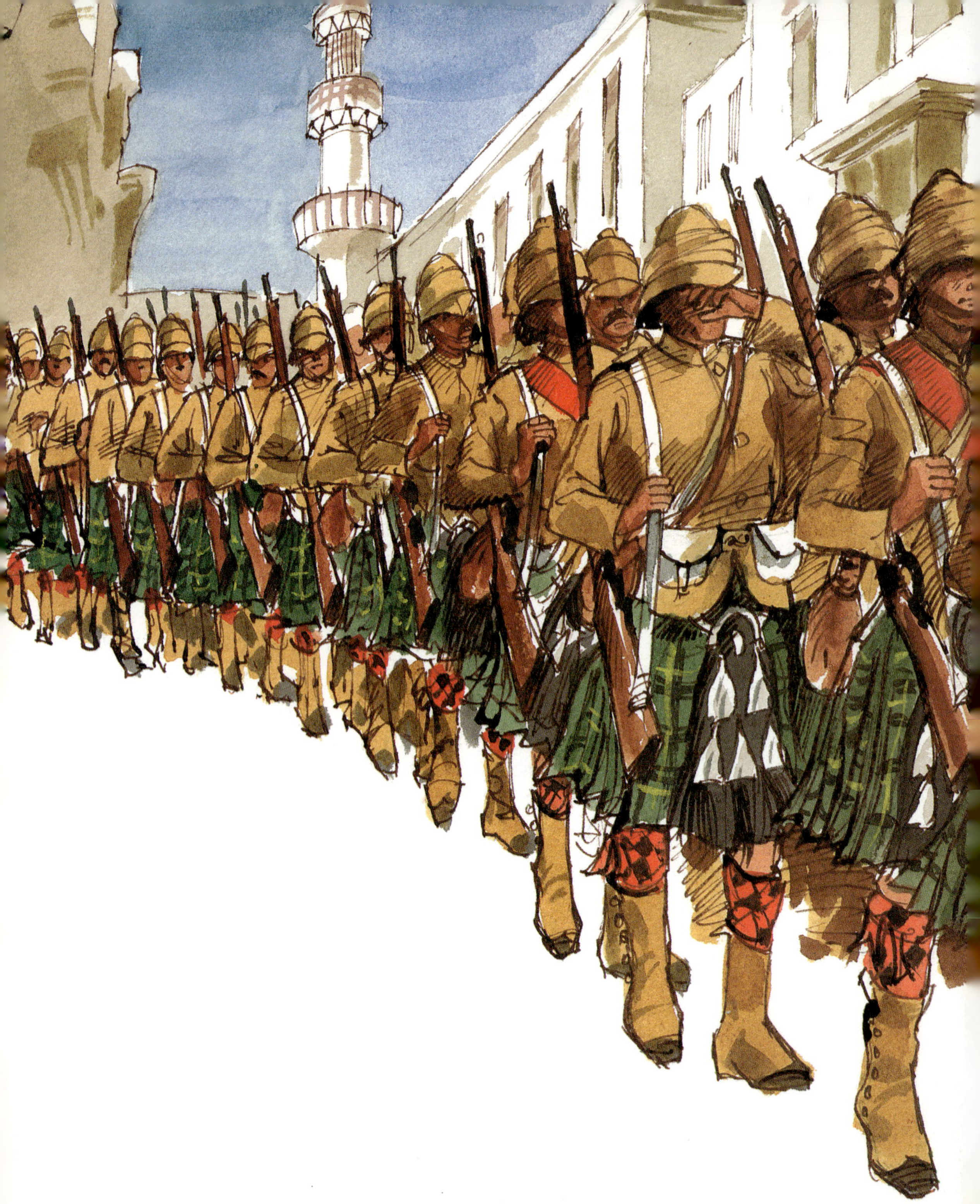

British occupation

As the column of British soldiers marched through Alexandria, a new recruit brushed the dust from his eyes. The sights and sounds that confronted him were difficult to understand. The soldier wondered what Britain wanted with such a place. He did not know that the eastern part of the British empire might well depend upon Britain's plans for Egypt.

Sir Garnet Wolseley and his army landed at Alexandria and moved quickly along the Suez Canal. The troops were soon on their way to At Tall al-Kabir, where they defeated the soldiers of Urabi. By the end of September 1882, Urabi had been arrested and put on trial by the British, acting for the khedive, Tawfiq. He was sentenced to exile from his country. Had Urabi been tried directly by the khedive or the forces of the Ottoman Empire, his fate might have been much worse. Nevertheless, their treatment of Urabi did not endear the British to the Egyptians. Egypt was still occupied by a foreign power, and not even a Muslim one at that.

The British occupation of Egypt altered the relationship between Egypt and Sudan, Egypt and Turkey, and Egypt and other Arabic-speaking members of the Ottoman Empire. It also created a bitter rivalry between England and France in Africa. But most important, it made Egyptians think more clearly about freedom from foreign rule. A true nationalist movement developed.

The Dufferin report

Lord Dufferin methodically wrote the last sentence on the sheet of paper. Finally, the report on the Egyptian situation was finished. Dufferin was pleased with his ideas about how the new government of Egypt under British supervision should be run. But he was not sure what the Egyptians would think about it. Still, he felt that the Egyptians would benefit from British laws, systems, and codes. Little did he know how resentful the Egyptians would become at Britain's interference and pompous attitudes.

The British sent Lord Dufferin, the British ambassador to the Ottoman Empire, to Egypt to report on what could be done to solve the country's political and financial problems

Lord Dufferin

Sir Evelyn Baring, El Lurd

after the Urabi Rebellion. In March 1883, Dufferin published his famous report. Britain's occupation of Egypt was supposed to be a short-term measure, but Dufferin made it clear that he believed Europeans should remain part of the country's administration for some time to come. In fact, Britain needed to protect its financial interests in Egypt and to ensure easy passage to eastern colonies through the Suez Canal. Britain was certainly not interested in making Egypt a better place for Egyptians.

Britain then sent Sir Evelyn Baring, Lord Cromer, better known to Egyptians as *El Lurd,* as consul general to put Dufferin's plans into action. Cromer was a colourless individual who approached everything as a bookkeeper might. But while Britons argued about what to do with Egypt, Cromer went about methodically making Egypt solvent and creating an orderly administration. In time, he put himself in the position of virtual ruler of Egypt, and by his refusal to act hastily, he convinced Britain that the rebuilding of Egypt would take a long time. He also managed to distance Egypt even further from Ottoman rule, as he would not tolerate interference from the empire or from France. Through Cromer, the British began to believe that they must remain in Egypt to keep others out.

Cromer managed to turn things around in a country that needed help. But his success was ultimately due to the fact that there was a British army in Egypt to back him up. In the end, his attitude further provoked Egyptian dislike of foreign rule, and made many Egyptians consider the possibility of self-rule.

Aswan

The men who had worked on the dam stood back in awe as the sluices opened and the first waters poured through. The dam looked magnificent and it would change the Nile Valley forever. No longer would the fellahin be at the mercy of the annual Nile flood. Now water could be stored behind the dam and used whenever it was needed.

For thousands of years, the present site of Aswan has been the gateway to Egypt from the south. It was the most southerly outpost of the pharaohs and the place where the arrival of the Nile floodwaters was signalled. It was here that engineers decided to erect the mighty dam that would conserve these floodwaters. Other economic development projects included improved irrigation and the building of barrages to help control the Nile.

The Aswan Dam was begun in 1898 and finished in 1902. It stretched across the Nile a distance of 2,152.5 metres, and after twice being heightened, in 1912 and 1934, it rose to 38 metres above its foundation. The reservoir capacity of the dam is an impressive 5.3 million cubic metres!

The dam made a great difference to farming in the Nile Valley. This increase in agricultural production helped the country on its way to recovery.

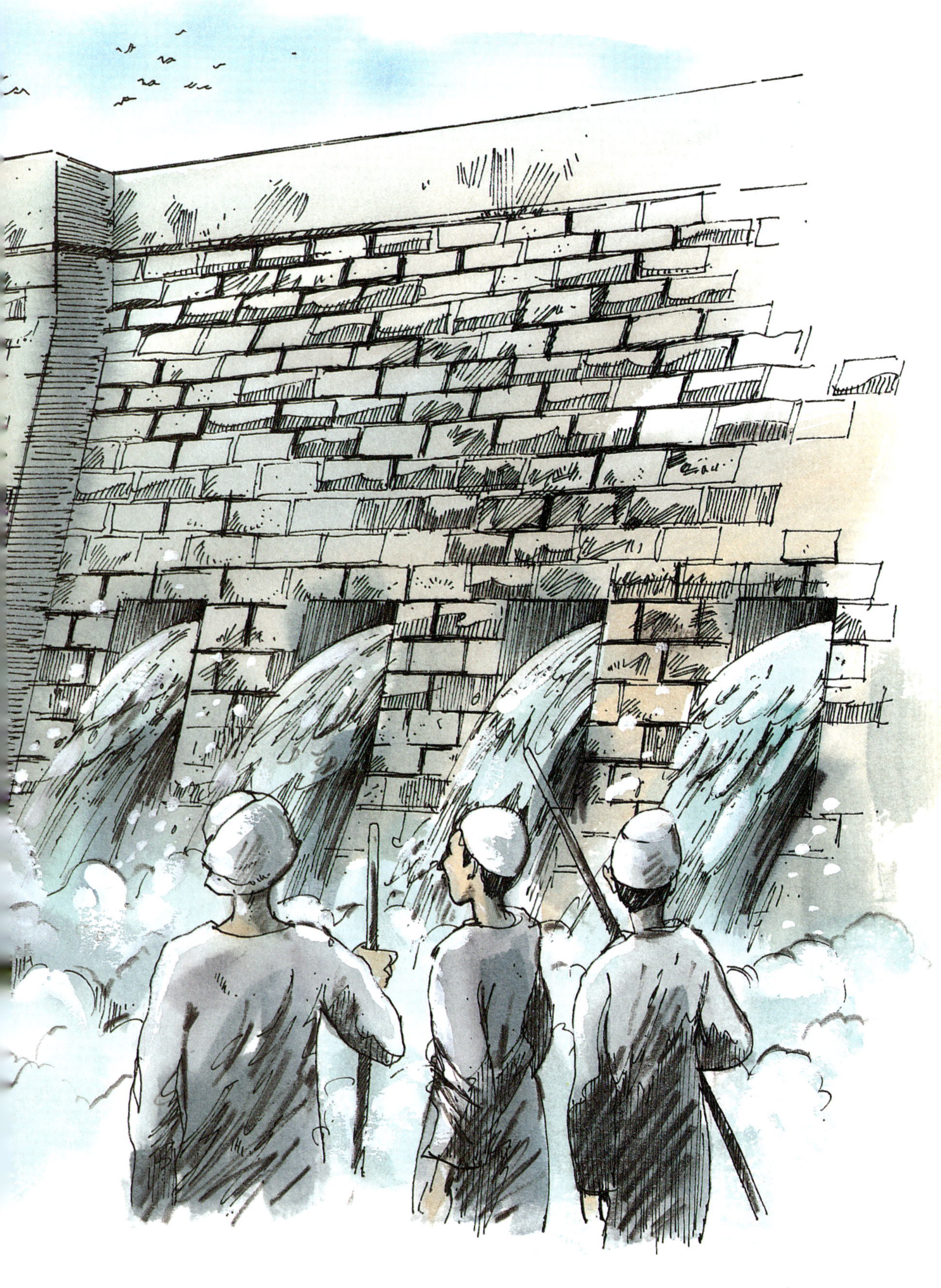

112

The siege of Khartoum

In 1881, a Sudanese leader called Mohammad Ahmad, who came to be known as the Mahdi, rose to power in the country. General Gordon, who arrived in Khartoum on February 18, 1884, offered terms of peace, but the Mahdi rejected them. Gordon and his men were besieged in Khartoum. They suffered attack after attack. Before long, their food supplies began to dwindle. The British government, led by Prime Minister William Gladstone, could not make up its mind what to do. Eventually, Gordon was killed. Khartoum fell and was occupied by rebels on January 23, 1885.

General Gordon

The Mahdi and Kitchener

Thinking they could seize Sudan now that Egyptian forces were being pulled out, the French had established a base at Fashoda.

For thirteen years, the Mahdi was in control of the Sudan. He revived the slave trade and posed a serious threat to the stability of Egypt. At last, Kitchener, the British general, was sent to Sudan to act as sirdar of the Egyptian army. The Anglo-Egyptian joint forces defeated the Mahdi's armies at the Battle of Omdurman in September 1898. Rather than chasing Mahdi forces, Kitchener headed towards Fashoda, where British and French forces came face to face. This led to the Fashoda crisis, which nearly caused war between Britain and France. Kitchener asked the French to leave Fashoda under the pretext that it was under Egyptian sovereignty. Following long negotiations, the French government ordered its forces in Fashoda to withdraw, which took place on November 4, 1898. In March 1895, a British-French agreement was concluded whereby their respective spheres of influence in Africa were defined.

The Sudan was restored on November 24, 1899, following more than three years of war in which the Egyptian army, assisted by some British units, fought. The Condominium Agreement of 1899 was subsequently concluded by Boutros Ghali on behalf of Egypt and Lord Cromer on behalf of Britain. Under this agreement the Governor General

Lord Kitchener of Khartoum

of the Sudan, the highest authority in the country, was a British official who held in hand all civil, military, executive, and legislative authorities. The Ottoman government protested that the British were interfering in matters falling within the sultan's exclusive authority, but it was not strong enough to dictate its will. By 1904, Britain and France had ended the long period of tension between them. Britain recognised France's claims to Morocco and France recognised Britain's claims to Egypt.

Mustafa Kamil and the first nationalists

Mustafa Kamil looked carefully at the front page of his paper, *Al Liwa (The Standard)*. The stories of the day fully expressed his feelings, both for Islam and for Egypt. He was particularly happy with the editorial that explained just why the British should leave his country.

Kamil was just one of a number of Egyptians who, in the late 1800's and early 1900's, spoke out for Egyptian and Islamic independence from Europe and the Ottoman Empire. Mustafa Kamil was the founder of the National Party and, between 1900 and 1907, editor of *Al Liwa,* which he used to outline his views on Egyptian and Islamic nationalism. He believed that Britain should evacuate Egypt, even if its removal required force on the part of the Egyptians. He felt strongly that Egypt should be governed by Egyptians and that Islam should not be influenced by the West.

Other men, such as Muhammad Abduh, Jamal al-Din al-Afghani, and Muhammad Rashid Rida, felt more or less the same way. Al-Afghani preached about the rational-scientific reform of Islam but was still faithful to the principles of the Islamic creed. Afghani also wanted to see the power of absolute rulers, like the sultan, restricted. His dream, though, was to see Islamic countries free from European control.

Muhammad Abduh was a disciple of Al-Afghani and the son of a Delta farmer. He trained to be an *alim* but was dismissed from his teaching post because of his association with al-Afghani. Then Khedive Tawfiq recalled Abduh to Cairo and made him editor of the *Official Gazette,* where he worked to reform education, language, and religion in Egypt. Exiled after the Urabi affair, he lived in Paris until returning to Egypt to take another position in the press. Continuing his work for reforms, he sought to improve the quality of written Arabic, the curriculum and administration of the education system, and religious practice and law. Abduh was interested more in justice than simply in the rules of a legal code. He was finally made mufti of Egypt—the supreme interpreter of the sharia. All his efforts, Abduh felt, would make Egypt a more modern country and therefore a country capable of self-government.

Muhammad Rashid Rida, Abduh's biographer and disciple, attempted to arrange Abduh's work into a system of religious thought. He founded the journal *Al-Manar* to voice Abduh's views.

The Ottomans

The Egyptian officer looked at the map of the Ottoman Empire. The empire was not as large as it used to be, he thought. It was in decline, and the officer, like many others in Egypt, felt that his country would be better off if it were no longer part of the empire. But the alternative was to give Europe even more power in Egypt, and the officer could not tolerate that either.

The Ottoman Empire had reached its peak during the reign of Sultan Suleiman I, who ruled from 1520 to 1566. By the 1800's the Ottoman Empire had become stagnant, and many nations had won independence from Ottoman rule. The weakened empire had little influence over many of its provinces. Thus, European powers were able to exert control over many areas of the Middle East.

In the 1800's, there was some reform of the educational system in the Ottoman Empire, but essentially the empire remained in the past. The glue that held the empire together was Islam, although the sultan/caliphs had been tolerant of non-Islamics, who had been allowed to live and worship as they saw fit.

After 1870, though, as the empire began to crumble, the sultan became less tolerant. Those in power thought that a stricter Islamic way of life might benefit the empire. But it did not. It served only to turn people against the sultan and to think more of independence from the empire. In fact, many thought the caliphate had fallen into disrepute under the sultan. Some even thought of establishing a separate Arab state.

Arab nationalists wanted to modernise Islam and the Islamic countries, including Egypt. But the sultan did not like the idea of modernisation and could not be persuaded to make changes that might benefit the Ottoman Empire. Thus, many intellectuals and political activists came to believe that it would be better to separate Arab provinces from the empire. They were aware that the European powers might not object to such a breakup. Nationalism was now becoming an important force.

Sinai: the Aqaba incident

The Turkish soldiers looked across the Sinai Peninsula. Years ago, soldiers protected pilgrims who went to and from Mecca across the peninsula, but today, they were here to support the railway line the sultan was building. They were also supporting the Ottoman sultan's claims to South Sinai, a parcel of land that had been ruled by Egypt until the Turks had moved in.

In theory, Sinai was part of the Ottoman Empire. But its borders had not been properly fixed, and from 1841 to 1892, no one had actually administered the area. Under the Khedive Tawfiq, however, it was agreed that South Sinai should be administered by Egypt. But when pilgrims no longer used this route to Mecca, the Ottomans decided they wanted the area back. The sultan had decided to extend the railway line from Maan to Aqaba, and sent troops to the garrison at Taba.

This move angered the British, who occupied Egypt, and they protested to the Ottoman sultan. Finally, the sultan gave way, and a new frontier was agreed on. It ran along a line from Rafa, on the Mediterranean coast, to a point 4.8 kilometres west of Aqaba. Thus, Taba remained in Egyptian territory, while Aqaba stayed Turkish.

The result of the Aqaba incident should have pleased the Egyptians, but many were not happy with it at all. They considered Britain's interference on their behalf humiliating because it emphasised Britain's control over Egypt.

The result was demonstrations, riots, and anti-British campaigns in the newspapers. The incident also stirred nationalistic feelings. Egyptians now believed that Egyptian territory should be negotiated for by a proper Egyptian government, answerable to no foreign power.

The peasants' cooperatives

Gamal looked sorrowfully at his wife. He had been the victim of some bad luck and had run into debt. His small farm produced just enough to sustain the family, and he could not yet pay the people he owed money to. Gamal felt lucky in one respect, however. Since the introduction of the Five Feddans Homestead Exemptions Law, his property could not be seized because of debt. He would have a chance of getting back on top of things. His father would not have been so fortunate.

The Five Feddans Homestead Exemptions Law was introduced by Lord Kitchener. Appointed to take over as consul general, Kitchener was more interested in the welfare of the fellahin than Cromer had been. Between 1907 and 1914, the first peasant cooperatives were established. The cooperatives were groups of fellahin who worked together to get the best use out of their land.

The Homestead Exemptions Law exempted from seizure for debts small holdings that did not exceed five feddans. Kitchener also induced the Egyptian government to initiate an anti-usury decree limiting interest on peasants' loans to 9 percent. The Five Feddans law aimed to give the fellahin a small holding, plus a water buffalo and a water wheel.

Such reforms did help the people of Egypt a little. But many still felt that the British did nothing to improve education. Certainly Egyptians were excluded from controlling their country. Nevertheless, Egypt began to prosper and standards of living rose for many.

A British protectorate

Ismail looked at the two men from the local authority and then across at the small farm he called his own. He wanted and needed to work on the farm, but the men said he could not. They told him he had to come with them and join the Egyptian Labour Corps. Ismail knew that the corps was organised to help the British in their war against the Germans. It was not his war. But he also knew that force would be used if he did not volunteer, so he would do as the men asked. Reluctantly, he joined the Egyptian Labour Corps, but he secretly hated the British for taking him away from his land.

The British were able to organise the Egyptian Labour Corps because in the late fall of 1914 they had made Egypt a *protectorate*. At war with Germany, Britain also declared war on Turkey when it became an ally of Germany. First Britain imposed martial law in Egypt, declaring that it would defend the country. Egyptians, however, would not have to fight; they simply had to avoid assisting the enemy. Then Britain declared Egypt a protectorate, or protected country, an act that effectively detached Egypt from Turkey.

This combination of martial law and protectorate status gave Britain virtually complete control over Egypt. Khedive Abbas was deposed and replaced by his uncle Hussein Kamel, who was given the title sultan rather than khedive. Kamel was the first Egyptian leader of his line not to be appointed by the Ottoman sultan. Next, the office of chief qadi of Egypt, a position held by Turks since the Ottoman conquest in 1517, was abolished.

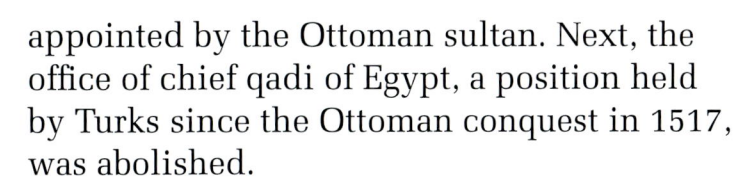

As the war went on and the fighting came closer to Egypt, thousands of troops arrived in the country from Britain, Australia, and other imperial nations. Their presence created huge problems for the Egyptians. The troops requisitioned buildings, recruited labour, and purchased and requisitioned animals and fodder. The Egyptian people began to feel they were, indeed, being forced into the war. The Egyptian Labour Corps and Camel Transport Corps, originally formed for railway construction, became more and more necessary to the war effort, and so more men were asked, or forced, to volunteer. The fellahin became angry at being forced to leave their land and to help fight against the caliph of Islam.

Some people made huge profits during the war, but the poor were suffering more than ever. They, as well as the middle-class, were ready to see the backs of the British and to welcome independence for their country.

After the war

Saad Zaghlul (*center*) was the leader of the Wafd. He came from a peasant family in Ibyanah and was educated at Al-Azhar. He became a judge, then minister of justice and minister of education. During the war he formed activist groups to promote Egyptian independence.

It was two days after the armistice that had ended World War I. Saad Zaghlul and two other former members of the Egyptian Legislative Assembly called on Sir Reginald Wingate, the British high commissioner. They demanded that the status of Egypt as a protectorate of Britain be ended. They wanted a treaty of alliance that would give Egypt its freedom as a sovereign state. But their demands went unheeded. The British were not yet ready to give up Egypt.

By the end of the war, the people of Egypt felt they had the right to be independent as well as to be represented at the peace conference. Saad Zaghlul and other members of the Wafd, a delegation formed as a voice for independence, approached Wingate to plead their case. Their requests were turned down, and they were refused permission to go to London to pursue their plan for independence. In fact, the British response was to declare martial law again. At the same time, Zaghlul was arrested and exiled to Malta. The result was more disturbances and revolts in Egypt. Now all classes of the population were involved.

Field Marshal Lord Allenby was sent by the British government to replace Wingate. Allenby was able to restore some order in the country. The situation was reassessed by the British, and as a result Zaghlul was allowed to leave Malta and attend the peace conference, although he was not given a hearing. Zaghlul then went to London to put forward the case for Egyptian independence. An agreement was even drafted, called the Milner-Zaghlul Agreement. However, Egypt could not agree to the obligations contained in it and Zaghlul was deported again, this time to the Seychelles. On February 28, 1922, Britain declared Egypt a sovereign state but kept control of the Suez Canal, the protection of foreign interests, the Nile waters, and Sudan. Prince Fuad, who had succeeded Hussein Kamel, then declared himself king and Egypt independent. The result, however, was only partial independence.

A sovereign state

Fuad I, King of Egypt, examined the document containing the details of his succession. He was pleased with it. His son would follow him as the next king, and then his son's son. The succession to the Egyptian throne would stay in his family. The former khedive, Abbas Hilmi, had been exiled, and he and his family had been excluded from any claim to the throne. Female members of the royal family were also excluded.

Fuad I was not content to be just a puppet king, however. He wanted a role in running the country. When the first constitution was shown to him, he rejected it because it reduced his power. A new constitution was drawn up that gave wider powers to the monarch. But these powers tended to weaken the authority of parliament and the cabinet. For instance, the king had the right to select and appoint the prime minister, to dismiss parliament, and to postpone parliamentary sessions. He also had the power to return new laws that he did not like to the government for reconsideration. This was more power than any European monarch had.

The power of the king was just one of the problems dogging Egypt's first years as a sovereign state. The British agreement to end its protectorate status did not allow real self-government, and unrest in the country continued for many years. When Saad Zaghlul was released from exile, he was able to take part in the first general election. His party, the Wafd, won by a convincing majority, and in 1924, Zaghlul became prime minister. But he could not control the anti-British violence he had helped promote and had to resign. His government lasted less than a year. Few governments after that lasted anywhere near their full term of office. In the meantime, Britain still held power over Egypt, keeping troops there to protect its interests along the Suez Canal.

Although this situation would not be resolved until 1952, Egypt had become the first Arab nation to achieve a measure of self-government.

Islam in Egypt

Egyptians are careful to perform their religious rites, especially prayers, at the specified times. To the Egyptian, prayers constitute an important part of life and are a duty to be carried out wherever he may be.

The Muslim faith, Islam, continues to be an important part of Egyptian life. In modern times, men like Gamal El Din Al Afghani and Muhammad Abdou called for adherence to the principles of Islam advocated by the Prophet Muhammad, Peace and Prayers be upon Him, and adopted by Muslims after him, for Islam is the faith that is compatible with the modern world.

Islam does not oppose reason or science, and so Muslims in Egypt readily take up the study of science. Today, the Higher Council of Islamic Research has decided on teaching modern humanities side by side with traditional subjects at Al Azhar.

When the Muslim countries came in contact with the West, problems began to emerge. While Muslims knew that Islam was not opposed to science, nor to modern approaches of seeking further knowledge, and though many regarded Western sciences worthy of study, there emerged a fanatic few who, having developed a faulty understanding of Islam and believing that it was opposed to Western thinking, rejected modern sciences. This was in contrast to the many who had welcomed and accepted such sciences. For this reason, Egyptian authorities have curbed the activities of these groups.

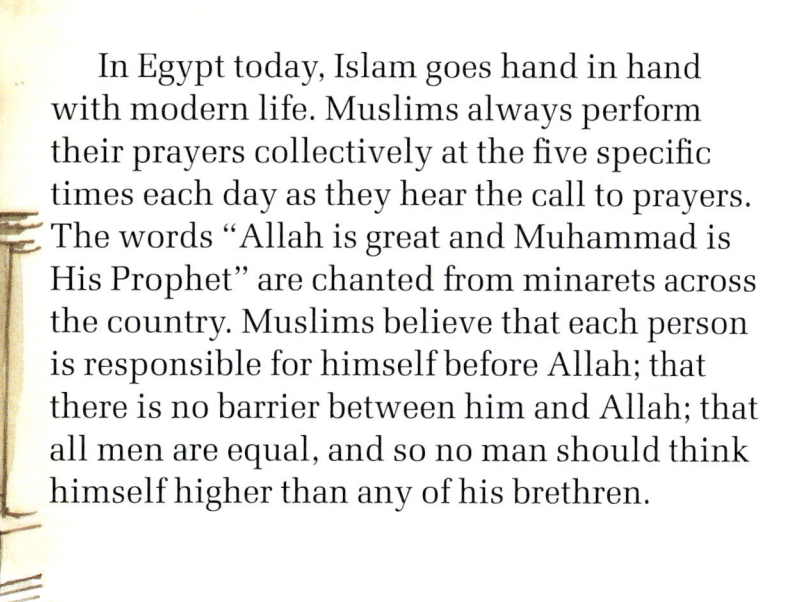

In Egypt today, Islam goes hand in hand with modern life. Muslims always perform their prayers collectively at the five specific times each day as they hear the call to prayers. The words "Allah is great and Muhammad is His Prophet" are chanted from minarets across the country. Muslims believe that each person is responsible for himself before Allah; that there is no barrier between him and Allah; that all men are equal, and so no man should think himself higher than any of his brethren.

Muslims also believe that all things are subject to Allah's will and are preordained by him. In Egypt, the words "en sha'a Allah," or "bi ithn Allah"—"if God wills or permits," are used by people instead of "yes."

Ramadan is celebrated in Egypt as in all Muslim countries. It is a lunar month during which Muslims fast from dawn to sunset.

Fear of Zionism

The reaction of the Arabs to the Jewish migration into British-held Palestine was rebellion. The position of the British in Palestine became impossible, and Britain resigned its mandate there to the United Nations. In 1947, the UN passed a Partition of Palestine Resolution, dividing the region into an Arab state and a Jewish state. The Egyptian delegation at the UN voted against the partition resolution, and the Egyptian government committed itself to participate in any Arab action against the resolution.

In the meantime, extremist groups in Egypt used the crisis to undermine the government. The Muslim Brotherhood tried to transform the Arab-Israeli conflict into an Arab-Islamic holy war against infidels.

On May 14, 1948, Israel declared itself an independent state. On May 15, Egyptian troops alongside troops from other Arab nations marched into Palestine. Their task was to try to prevent the establishment of the Israeli state. At the same time, acts of violence were carried out against Jewish and foreign targets in Egypt. An explosion in the Jewish sector of Cairo killed more than ten people. But the Palestine situation had caused martial law to be declared in Egypt, and steps were taken to stop the horrors.

Hostilities in Palestine finally came to an end. Egypt signed an armistice agreement with Israel in February 1949. Entanglements and wars continued afterwards, leading to further bloodshedding. Then, events took another path, until the peace treaty was signed in 1979.

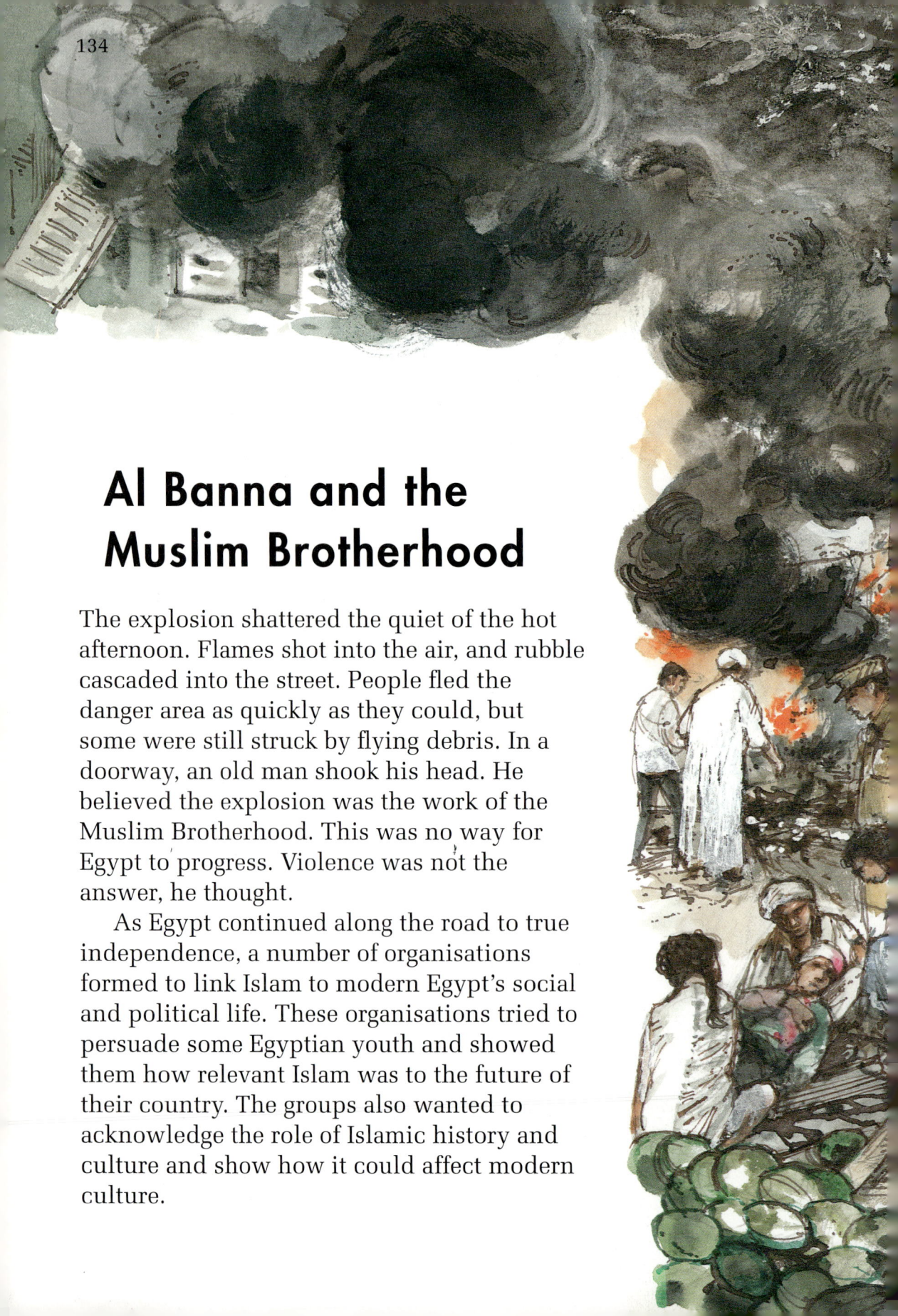

Al Banna and the Muslim Brotherhood

The explosion shattered the quiet of the hot afternoon. Flames shot into the air, and rubble cascaded into the street. People fled the danger area as quickly as they could, but some were still struck by flying debris. In a doorway, an old man shook his head. He believed the explosion was the work of the Muslim Brotherhood. This was no way for Egypt to progress. Violence was not the answer, he thought.

As Egypt continued along the road to true independence, a number of organisations formed to link Islam to modern Egypt's social and political life. These organisations tried to persuade some Egyptian youth and showed them how relevant Islam was to the future of their country. The groups also wanted to acknowledge the role of Islamic history and culture and show how it could affect modern culture.

The most important of these societies was the Muslim Brotherhood. It was a militant political organisation that promoted an Islamic government and was willing to use force to achieve it. The Brotherhood began as a Muslim association content with religious teaching. Its founder, Hassan al Banna, however, styled himself the Supreme Guide who would, one day, lead the faithful in a purified Muslim state. This idea appealed to a growing number of members. The Brotherhood also scorned European culture and moral values, and thought that these values should be removed from Egyptian life altogether.

Throughout the 1930's, the Muslim Brotherhood agitated against foreign schools and other European institutions. It called for stronger cooperation with other Arab states against Zionism in Palestine.

In time, the Brotherhood became more than just an Egyptian organisation. It operated in Syria and Jordan, and supported similar groups in Pakistan and Iran. Unfortunately, its members' fanatical beliefs and paramilitary training led to acts of terrorism. Governments began to use repressive police methods against the Brotherhood as well as against other, less dangerous groups. Further chaos resulted within the country.

Finally, during the conflict in Palestine, with martial law in operation, the Muslim Brotherhood was ordered to disband. Twenty days later, one of its members murdered Nuqrashi, the prime minister. Later Hassan al Banna himself would be murdered by unknown assassins.

Republic

For many years, British control of the Egyptian army had stopped. But the breakdown of order in Egypt during 1950 and 1951 created the perfect opportunity for rebellion among the army officer corps and units. The younger, junior officers blamed the government and the king for their defeat in Palestine. They felt it was time to do something about the situation in Egypt. Nine of these officers organised themselves in September 1949 into the so-called Constituent Committee of Free Officers. The group included Colonel Gamal Abdel Nasser and Colonel Anwar el-Sadat.

For two years, the group recruited a number of officers sympathetic to their cause. Through the press and civilian groups they campaigned against the rulers in Egypt and were able to have control over the Board of the Officers Club—an important institution in the army in the December 31, 1951, elections in which all nominees of the Free Officers defeated all nominees of the Royal Palace. The elections were a blow to the monarch, who saw in the activities of the Free Officers a real threat.

To counteract the success of the Free Officers and to reassert his control over the army, King Faruk made his brother-in-law, Ismail Sherine, minister of war in Naguib El-Hilali Cabinet, which was formed on July 22, 1952. But Faruk's attempts were futile.

The Free Officers discounted the possibility of a counter move by the British troops stationed in the Canal Zone because of the deterioration of the political situation in Egypt in the aftermath of the burning of Cairo and because King Faruk's stature had been undermined by reason of his and his family's scandals and also because some members of his entourage were accused of charges in the defected arms affair.

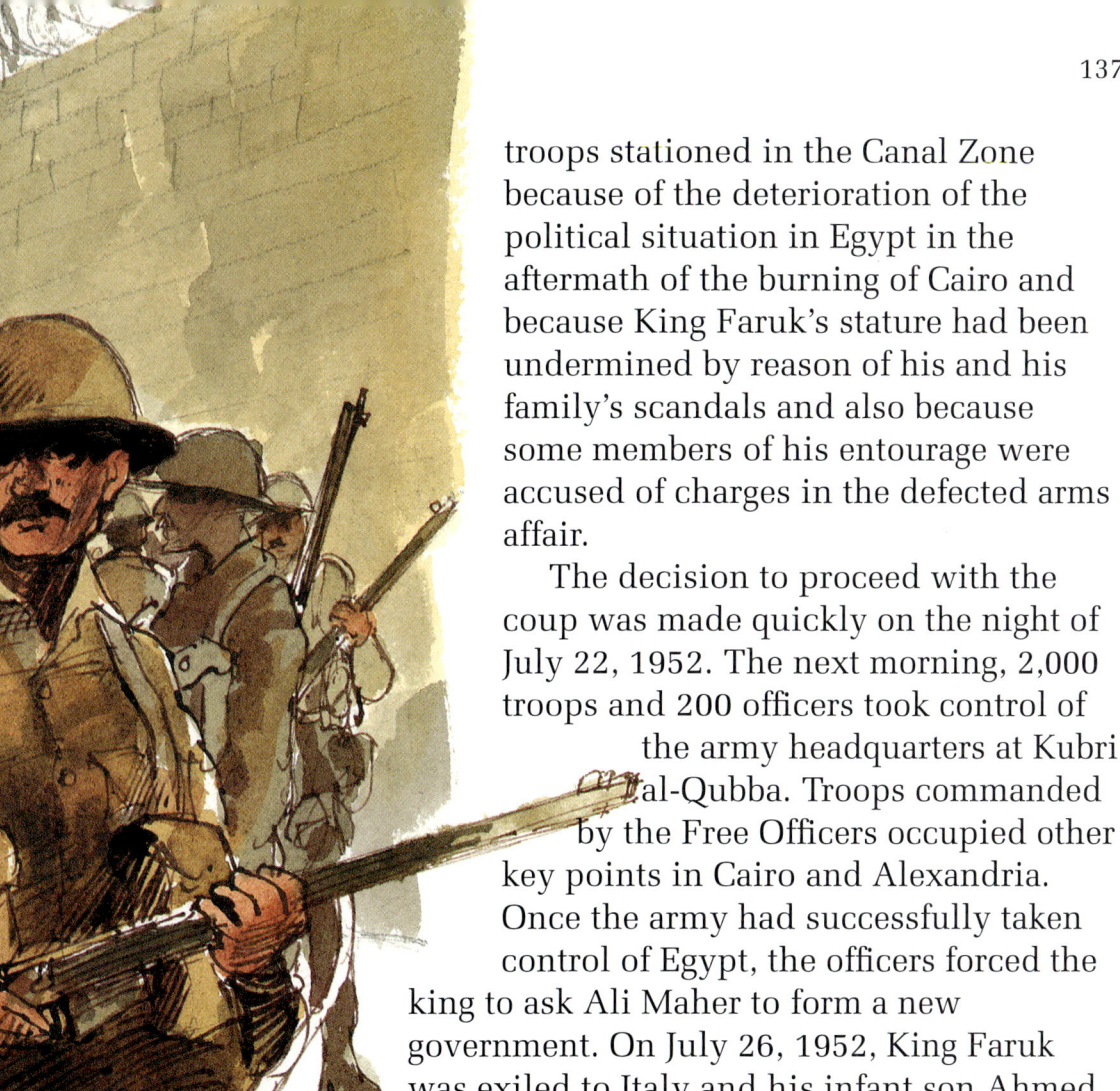

The decision to proceed with the coup was made quickly on the night of July 22, 1952. The next morning, 2,000 troops and 200 officers took control of the army headquarters at Kubri al-Qubba. Troops commanded by the Free Officers occupied other key points in Cairo and Alexandria. Once the army had successfully taken control of Egypt, the officers forced the king to ask Ali Maher to form a new government. On July 26, 1952, King Faruk was exiled to Italy and his infant son Ahmed Fuad declared king under a Regency Council. In January 1953, all political parties were banned. On June 18, 1953, the army rulers, now known as the Revolutionary Command Council, declared Egypt a republic. The monarchy was abolished and Muhammad Naguib became the first president of the Republic.

King Faruk

The former king Faruk looked back at the seafront of Alexandria and felt both sad and angry. Faruk was on board his yacht, *Mahroussa,* and leaving the country. He had been ordered by the new army rulers of Egypt to abdicate. His infant son, Prince Ahmed Fuad, had been proclaimed king in his place, and a Regency Council was set up to look after his interests. For most of his term as king, Faruk had been at odds with the government. Now the government leaders were congratulating the army for ridding the country of the "tyrant" Faruk.

Faruk became king of Egypt on the death of his father, Fuad, in 1936. He immediately carried on the old fight of his father against the Wafd, which he viewed as a major competitor for power in the country. Members of the Wafd felt that they could deal easily with the young, inexperienced, and poorly educated king. But they did not take into account the forces Faruk could bring to his aid, including religious leaders, courtiers, minor party politicians who were opposed to the Wafd, and, for some years, the army. Having such allies put the king in a position of power that did little to help the progress of representative government in Egypt.

This struggle for power between the government and the monarchy continued until the military coup of 1952 and the deposition of the king. Faruk quarrelled not only with his own government but also with the British. And during World War II (1939–1945), when fighting occurred in Egypt and the Middle East, Faruk was sympathetic to the Axis powers—the enemies of Britain and the West. This situation caused a serious threat to security in Egypt as far as the British were concerned. The king, however, was interested in keeping Egypt out of the war. Nevertheless, when the war in North Africa became difficult enough for Britain to intervene in Egyptian affairs in 1942, the king had no choice but to do as the British wanted—in this case to allow the formation of a Wafd government that would be better for Britain's interests in Egypt. As a result, the rift between Faruk and the Wafd opened even further. The king, in fact, had been humiliated. The situation became worse as the war trundled to an end and Wafdist leaders argued among themselves. The king, no longer fearful of British interference, conspired to dismiss the Wafd prime minister, and the party was removed from power.

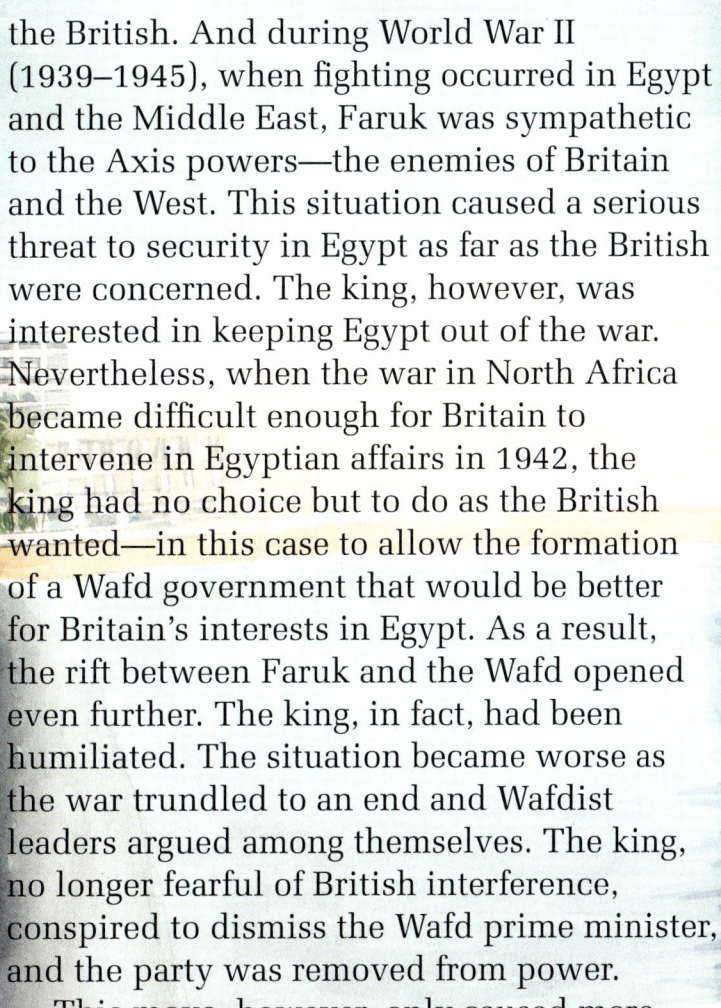

This move, however, only caused more discontent in Egypt, and it became clear that no one was really in control. Over the next few postwar years, even the army, which had been loyal to the king, began to grumble. Faruk was overconfident that the army would support him and too dependent on some of his officer cronies. A group of army officers, who became known as the Free Officers, challenged the king's control over the army and were successful. Their final act was the coup of July 23, 1952, when the Free Officers took control of Egypt and forced Faruk to abdicate the throne.

Egypt ruled by an Egyptian

The rich landowner looked at the great tract of land that he had called his own. Now it was to be broken up and distributed to other people. According to President Nasser, no one was to hold more than 200 feddans of land. The rich landowner held over 1,000 feddans and so would lose most of his estate.

The reallocation of land was just one of the actions taken by the Revolutionary Command Council. A new constitution was issued on January 16, 1956, and the people were invited to a referendum on June 25, 1956, concerning the new constitution and the presidency. Abdul Nasser was chosen by an overwhelming majority and thereby became president of the republic. Accordingly, the Revolutionary Command Council was disbanded, and Abdul Nasser held the legitimate authority in the country.

Abdul Nasser was born in 1918 in a mud-brick house on an unpaved street in the Bacos section of Alexandria. He went to school in Cairo, where he found himself constantly in trouble with teachers—mostly British. Young Nasser also took part in many anti-British street demonstrations. After a few months at law school, he attended the military college and graduated as an officer in the Egyptian army. Nasser led the Free Officers in the coup that toppled the Egyptian monarchy and placed the army in control of the country. One of Nasser's first acts was to reallocate land. He wanted all peasants to own their own land and

Gamal Abdul Nasser

stipulated that no one should hold more than 200 feddans. Later, landowners would be limited to 100 feddans. This policy broke up large estates but also resulted in the destruction of cattle herds because the poorer farmers could not afford to keep them.

Under Nasser, Egypt went to war in Yemen, causing great loss of life as well as money. The United States, upset by the policies Egypt was following, cut its economic aid. Nasser turned more and more to the U.S.S.R. for help. Another war with Israel on June 5, 1967, ended in failure, and Nasser resigned. But he was so popular that people turned out in the thousands to support him. Their refusal to accept his resignation was a measure of his extraordinary appeal.

The Suez crisis

People were shouting and dancing in the streets of Cairo, Alexandria, and most of the larger cities. On July 26, 1956, President Nasser had announced the news of nationalising the Suez Canal Company, which had been controlled by the British and French. However, the British and French were furious. They had lost their lifeline for oil supplies to Europe.

Nasser seized the canal because Britain and the United States refused to help finance the new Aswan High Dam, which would more than double Egypt's fertile land.

The seizure of the canal led a group of countries to put together a plan for the international control of it. Britain and France threatened military action if Nasser did not accept the plan. Nasser, nevertheless, rejected it. On October 29, 1956, Israeli troops surged into Egypt across the Sinai Desert. They claimed it was a reprisal for attacks on them. It did not take long before the plot connived by Britain, France, and Israel against Egypt was revealed. On October 30, Britain and France dispatched a warning to both Egypt and Israel, calling for the withdrawal of all their military forces 10 miles (16 kilometers) away from the Suez Canal, and demanding that Egypt would accept the occupation of the main locations in Port Said, Ismailia, and Suez by British and French troops. Israel accepted, of course, but Nasser discarded the warning. The British embarked on bombarding several vital targets in Cairo and some canal cities, and shoved their troops from Malta and Cyprus towards Egypt. Then, the British and French troops attacked Port Said and Port Fouad on November 5, 1956. The utmost point achieved by the aggressors was "Cap," 22 miles (35 kilometers) south of Port Said. In response to the UN resolution to stop their aggression, Britain, France, and Israel issued their orders to their troops to cease fire. All military operations stopped as of the morning of November 7, 1956, due to the persuasion of the UN and the United States to stop the aggression and to replace the aggressive troops with international UN troops. Further pressure was exerted by the U.S.S.R. and the United States to impel Britain and France to pull out their troops from Egypt.

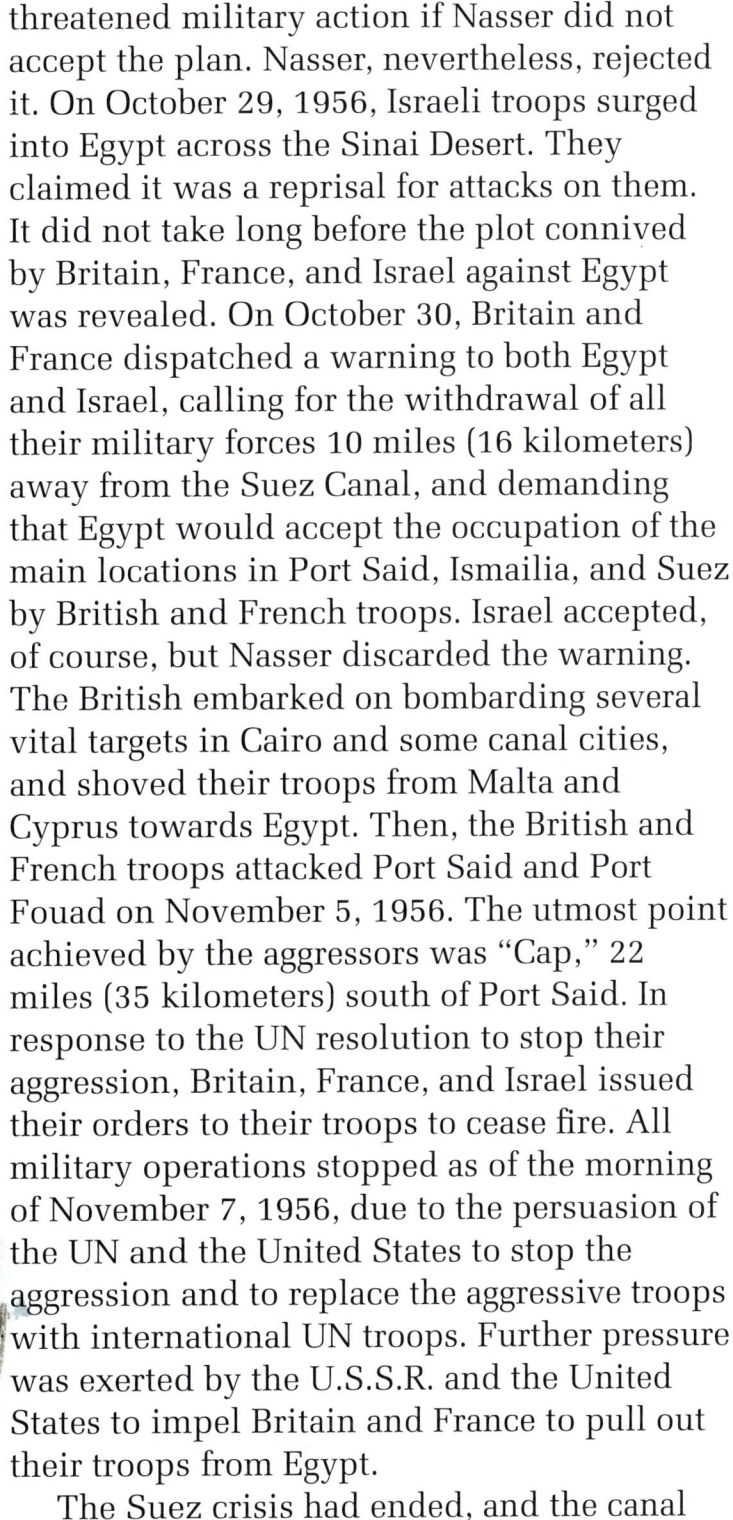

The Suez crisis had ended, and the canal became free for shipping again.

Egypt at war

The lone herdsman stood behind a large outcropping of rock and watched the tanks as they rolled relentlessly across the desert. The tanks were Egyptian, and they were heading for Israeli posts across the Sinai. If the assault was quick and decisive, the Egyptians would have a huge advantage.

It was October 1973. The Egyptians had learned from the defeat inflicted upon them by the Israelis in the Six-Day War and were much better prepared and equipped than they had been in 1967. The assault on the Israeli forces took place on Yom Kippur, the holiest day of the Jewish calendar. It caught the Israelis unprepared. Anwar el-Sadat's success won him support from other Arab countries. However, the Israeli army was resupplied by the United States. This backing given to the Israeli army eventually enabled it to chase Egyptian forces beyond the Suez Canal. The war drew the attention of the United States to the need for stability in the Middle East. And Anwar el-Sadat emerged as a powerful Egyptian leader.

In 1974, Egypt and Israel agreed to separate their forces in the Sinai. Then a year later, Israel agreed to remove its troops from a part of the Sinai it had occupied since 1967. Finally, in June 1975, the Suez Canal, which had been closed since the Six-Day War, was reopened.

Map of war area

Mediterranean Sea
Gaza Strip
Israel
Suez Canal
Jordan
Sinai Peninsula
Egypt

Anwar el-Sadat (*left*), Jimmy Carter (*center*), and Menachem Begin (*right*) met at Camp David in September 1978.

Camp David

President Jimmy Carter of the United States looked on as Israeli Prime Minister Menachem Begin spoke with President Anwar el-Sadat. Carter was pleased to see the two men sitting together and trying to resolve the differences their two countries had with each other. If an agreement could be made, it would be an historic occasion.

The meeting took place at Camp David in the United States. The year before, President Sadat had made an unprecedented trip to Israel to talk to the Israeli Knesset, or parliament. "No more war; no more bloodshed" was the slogan of the meeting. Sadat declared that he wanted a permanent peace arrangement for the Middle East. The Israelis also wanted peace badly, although it would mean withdrawing from territory they had conquered during the 1967 war. Happily, both parties agreed to continue their talks.

As a result of Sadat's trip to Israel, he and Israeli Prime Minister Menachem Begin agreed to meet in the United States at Camp David, along with President Jimmy Carter. On September 18, 1978, Sadat and Begin announced that they had reached an agreement on the signing of a peace treaty. It was a political triumph for both leaders, and it opened the door for Egypt and Israel to settle their differences away from the battlefield. The agreement was called the Camp David Accords and was the first such agreement between Israel and an Arab nation. It guaranteed the return of the Sinai to Egypt and called for a peace treaty to be signed between the two countries. The treaty was signed in 1979.

Sadat had solved one problem but created others. His policies and his agreement with Israel were not well accepted by other Arab states nor by fundamentalists in his own country. Egypt was removed from the Arab League, and some Arab countries broke off diplomatic relations with Egypt. Discontent in the country grew as prosperity did not follow the signing of the accord. Then, on October 6, 1981, as President Sadat watched a parade in Cairo, he was assassinated by extremists.

President Sadat and Prime Minister Begin were each awarded the Nobel Peace Prize for their work in making peace between their two countries.

After Sadat

The small boy tried to hurry through the Cairo streets to finish his errand. But there were so many people that he could hardly move. So many people, he thought. One day there would be too many people for the city. The boy had heard that the population of Cairo was over 10 million. He could not imagine such a figure. But it must surely be true, judging from all the people who crowded the streets.

One problem facing Hosni Mubarak, president of Egypt, was that Egypt's population was simply too great for Egypt's resources. Not only that, but also the population continued to grow. Better irrigation could solve part of the problem, but Egypt still relied on the Nile, especially as the Aswan High Dam did not solve all problems of Egypt. Egypt also had to contend with natural disasters. In 1992, an earthquake struck Cairo, killing nearly 368 people and causing a billion dollars in property damage.

In other respects, Mubarak's Egypt progressed. Mubarak himself proved a popular leader. He was less outspoken than Anwar el-Sadat on many controversial issues and tried to rebuild Egypt's relationship with other Arab nations. Mubarak's Egypt was very important not only to the Egyptians but also to the United States and the former U.S.S.R. and other countries. Everybody saw Egypt as a strategic region in the Middle East. Thus, Egypt was provided with economic and military aid.

When Iraq invaded Kuwait in 1990, Egypt took a leading role in Arab opposition to the invasion. When the Gulf War finally began, Egypt joined a coalition that included the United States, Saudi Arabia, and other nations. Thousands of Egyptian troops took part in the allied offensive, including the bombing of Iraqi strongholds. Egypt has had to fight violence from within, as well as outside, the country. In the early 1990's there was a further outbreak of violence by some extremist youth. The government confronted such actions with the utmost firmness and force, until security and safety prevailed once again.

Village life

The young woman carefully took the bread out of the oven in the courtyard of her house. Her husband worked in the fields from sunup until midday. He would expect her to bring bread as well as tomatoes or a cucumber for him to eat.

Villagers in Egypt live much as they have for hundreds of years. Their houses are usually of one or two storeys made of mud bricks. They are mud plastered or whitewashed. In some, a staircase on the outside leads to a flat roof, where the owners sleep in summer. Around the house is a courtyard, with perhaps a small garden. Some houses display painted scenes of boats, trains, camels, or mosques to show that the owner has made a pilgrimage to Mecca. One of the largest houses in the village belongs to the *omdeh,* or headman, of the village.

Most villages now have piped water. If a village does not, water comes from a well or the river. It is carried in a two-handled jar called a *bolas* and stored inside the house in a porous jar buried halfway to keep it cool. Each village has a tailor and a seamstress for making clothes. Material for the clothes is bought in the nearest town from travelling salesmen. Donkey carts transport goods such as tinware for cooking, washing, and storage, and groceries of different kinds. Where there is no electricity, kerosene is brought in to fuel primus stoves, storm lanterns, and pressure lamps.

Most villages have a clinic and a well-qualified doctor. Every medical graduate in Egypt is required to serve some time in a village clinic.

Many fellahin own a small amount of land. This land enables them to grow vegetables for themselves and maize to feed their animals. Most families keep a donkey, some hens, and ducks, and possibly a turkey. A water buffalo is highly prized.

The men work in the fields from early morning until noon. They then have a meal of bread, vegetables, and tea. Many fellahin are employed on larger farms and farm their own land in the evening and on weekends. Most work a seven-day week.

The Arts

The arts are as important in modern Egypt as they were in ancient times. Egypt has produced many great artists, of whom the most famous is probably the writer Naguib Mahfouz.

Mahfouz was born the son of a civil servant and attended Cairo University before going to work in the civil service himself. He retired in 1971. His first novels, such as *Radabis,* were set in ancient Egypt. But later Mahfouz turned to modern Egypt for his themes. He was able to depict in his novels the true flavour of life among the city poor in Egypt, which made him very popular. His major work, *Al Thula Thiya,* known as the Cairo Trilogy, describes families who lived in Cairo from World War I until 1952. Mahfouz wrote some 40 novels and short story collections, as well as 30 screenplays and several plays. He was awarded the Nobel Prize for literature in 1988—the first Arab writer to be so honoured.

Omm Kulthuum

Naguib Mahfouz

Egyptian cinema is popular throughout the Arab world.

   Urban poverty is a recurring theme in Egyptian literature. Another often-used theme is the impact of the West and Europe upon Egyptian life. This is exemplified in the novel *The Bird from the East,* by another gifted Egyptian writer, Tawfiq al-Hakim.

   Music has a long tradition in Egypt. Popular Egyptian music includes folk music of the country, traditional Arabic music, and Western-style music. Perhaps the country's most famous singer is Omm Kulthuum. Her voice has been celebrated in Egypt and other Arabic-speaking countries for over 50 years.

   Film making is also important in modern Egypt, dating back to a period before World War I. The founding of the Misr Studios in 1934, however, stimulated the growth of the industry, and today modern Egyptian films are shown all over the Arab world. There are many private film companies as well as the state-owned Egyptian General Cinema Corporation.

Special Words

adze   An ax-like tool with an arched blade used for carving wood.

akh   One of the components of the human personality as understood by the ancient Egyptians. When united after death, the ka and the ba became an entity called the akh.

archaic   Ancient; referring to an early period in the history of a culture.

ba   An ancient Egyptian word corresponding to the idea of the soul. One of the elements of the human personality.

Bedouin   A nomadic Arab of the desert.

caliph   The ruler of Islam.

cartouche   An elongated loop, or oval, that contains the last two names of an Egyptian ruler.

cataract   A large, steep waterfall.

citadel   A fortress, usually found on high ground, that protects a city or town.

Coptic   The final stage of the ancient Egyptian language, and that used by the first Egyptian Christians. It is now used only as the language of the Coptic church.

dynasty   A series of rulers who belong to the same family.

feddan   An area of land equalling 1.038 acres.

fellah   An Egyptian peasant or laborer. The plural of *fellah* is *fellahin*.

hieroglyph   A picture used to represent a word, sound, or idea in a pictorial system of writing called hieroglyphics.

Islam   A word that means "submission." It refers to the Muslim faith established by the prophet Muhammad.

ka   An ancient Egyptian word meaning a manifestation of the energy of life; one of the elements of the human personality. It was the term for the human double to which offerings were made.

Kaaba	A building at Mecca containing the Muslims' sacred black stone. It is cube-shaped and covered by a large black cloth. It is said to have been built by Abraham.
khedive	A title given to the rulers of Egypt by the Ottoman Sultan. It is similar to the title "prince."
Mameluke	A word which means "owned" but refers to soldiers who began their careers as slaves and eventually rose to rule Egypt.
mastaba	An Arabic word meaning "bench," which archaeologists use to describe private tombs of the Old Kingdom.
Muslim	One who submits. A follower of Islam.
nomarch	A governor of a nome, or province, of Egypt under the Greek pharaohs. There were 42 nomes in Egypt during the late period.
Omdah	The headman in a modern Egyptian village.
oracle	A place where gods were consulted for advice or prophesy.
papyrus	An aquatic, or water, plant of the sedge family. The ancient Egyptians used the plant to make a writing material like paper. Papyrus was also used in boat-building.
pharaoh	A word meaning "great house," but which came to mean the ruler, or king, of ancient Egypt.
Quraysh	An ancient aristocratic tribe of the Arabian Peninsula.
sarcophagus	A stone coffin.
satrapy	A province of the Persian Empire. The governor of the province was called a satrap.
Shiite	A member of a Muslim sect that believes the Islamic ruler should be a direct descendant of the prophet Muhammad.
sultan	A Turkish word meaning "ruler."
vizier	A chief minister.
Wafd	An Egyptian nationalist group that became a political party.

Index

This index is an alphabetical list of the important words and topics in this book.

When you are looking for a special piece of information, you can look for the word in this list and it will tell you which pages to look at.

Abbas, Khedive 125
Abbas I 102
Abbasid caliphate 79
Abduh, Muhammad 117, 119
Abu Simbel 49 (illus)
Abydos 19, 49
Afghani, Jamal al-Din al- 117, 119
agriculture
   under Nasser 140–141
   peasants' cooperatives 122–123
   Roman times 68–69
Ahmose, admiral of Thutmose I 34
Ahmose I 33, 35 (illus)
akh 27
Akhenaton 35, 40–41
al Banna, Hassan. See Banna, Hassan al
Alexander the Great 60–61
Ali Bey 92–93
Allenby, Lord 127
Al-Qahirah 79
Amarna revolution 40–41
Amenhotep III 35 (illus), 38
Amon 24–25, 57
Amr ibn el-As 77
Anubis 24–25 (illus)
Aqaba incident 120–121
Arab League 147
Archaic Period 15
arts 152–153

Astarte 33
astronomy 46–47
Aswan Dam 110–111, 148
Aton 40–41
At Tall al-Kabir 107
Avaris 33
Aybak 85
Ayyubid dynasty 82–83

ba 27
Badarian culture 8
Banna, Hassan al 135
Baring, Sir Evelyn, Lord Cromer 109 (illus)
Baybars 85, 86–87
Bedouins 77
Begin, Menachem 146–147
Bible 38–39
boats 50–51 (illus)
Byzantine empire 77

Caesar, Julius 66–67
Cairo 82–83. See also Al-Qahirah
calendar 47
Cambyses 58–59
Camp David Accords 146–147
Carter, Howard 42–43
Carter, Jimmy 144–145
cartouches 55
Champollion, Jean-François 55
Cheops (Khufu) 22, 23

children 44–45
Christians
   Copts 72–73
   crusades 80–81
Cleopatra VII 20, 66–67
Constantinople 80
cooperatives 122–123
Coptic language 72–73
Copts 72–73
cotton industry 100–101
creation story 24–25
Cromer, Lord (Evelyn Baring 109 (illus)
crowns 15 (illus)
crusades 80–81

de Lesseps, Ferdinand 102–103
Delta, Nile 6
Demetrius Phalerus 64
demotic writing 55
Diocletian 71
double crown 15 (illus)
Dufferin report 108–109
dynasties of ancient Egypt 21
   Archaic Period 15
   dynasties XXII-XXVII 58–59
   First Intermediate Period 30
   Middle Kingdom 30–31
   New Kingdom 34–35
   Old Kingdom 20–21

Second Intermediate
 Period 32–33

education 54–55, 97
Egyptian Labour Corps 125
eighteenth dynasty 34–35
everyday life
 ancient Egypt 44–45
 Egypt today 150–151
 Ottoman Egypt 90–91

Faruk I 137, 138–139
Fashoda 114
Fatimids 78–79
fellahin
 in ancient Egypt 16
 under British occupation
  122–123
 in Egypt today 150–151
 under Mamelukes 85
 in Ottoman Empire 90–91
filmmaking 152
First Cataract 6
First Intermediate Period 30
Five Feddans Homestead
 Exemptions Law 122–123
flint tools 8 (illus)
flood 6–7, 47
 and Aswan Dam 110–111
food 45. See also Agriculture
Free Officers movement
 136–137, 139
Fuad I 127, 128–129
funerals 26–27
 Opening of the Mouth
  ceremony 56–57

games 45
Geb 24 (illus)
gods 24–25, 40–41. See
 also Religion
Gordon, General Charles
 George 113 (illus)
government
 after unification 10–11
 Fuad I 128–129

khedive 104
 under Muhammad Ali
  98–99
 under Napoleon 95
 priests 56–57
Great Britain
 occupation 107, 108–109
 protectorate 124–125,
  126–127
Greek rulers of Egypt 64–65

Hakim, Tawfiq al- 152
Hatshepsut 35, 36–37
Heliopolis 46–47
Hierakonpolis 16
hieratic writing 55
hieroglyphics 54–55
Hittites 48–49
Homestead Exemptions Law
 123
Horus 12–13, 24
Horus name 22
Hyksos 32–33

ibn Talun 78–79
Ibrahim 102
Ikhshidid dynasty 79
Institut Français 94–95
Inundation. See Flood
irrigation 16
Isis 12, 24–25 (illus)
Islam 74–75, 130–131
Ismail 103
Israel 133, 143, 146–147

Jamal al-Din al-Afghani.
 See Afghani, Jamal al-Din
 al-
Joseph 38–39

ka 26–27
Kamel, Hussein 125
Kamil, Mustafa 116–117
Kamose 33
Karnak 49
Khartoum, siege of 113

Khnum 26
Khufu (Cheops) 22, 23
Kitchener, Lord Herbert 114
 (illus), 123
Koran 75
Kulthum, Omm 152
Kush. See Nubia

land reform
 under British 122–123
 under Nasser 140–141
library at Alexandria 64–65
Libyan dynasties 58
lighthouse of Alexandria 63
Lower Egypt 8. See also
 Delta, Nile
Luxor. See Thebes

Mahdi 113 (illus), 114
Mahfouz, Naguib 152
Mamelukes 84–85
 Ali Bey 92–93
Manetho 20–21
maps
 Egypt 7
 Upper and Lower Egypt 11
 Yom Kippur War 145
Mark, Saint 72–73
Mark Antony 67
mastaba tomb 18–19 (illus)
Mastansir, al 87
Memphis 15, 18–19, 25,
 32–33
Menes 14–15
Mentuhotep I 30–31 (illus)
Middle Kingdom 30–31
military coup of 1952
 136–137, 138–139
Milner-Zaghlul Agreement
 127
Mongols 87
mosques 83
Mubarak, Hosni 148–149
Muhammad Ali 96–97
Muhammad the prophet
 74–75

mummification 28–29 (illus)
music 152
Muslim Brotherhood 130, 132, 134–135

Naguib, Muhammad 137
name 27
Napoleon 94–95
Naqada cultures 8–9
Narmer palette 15
Nasser, Gamal Abdel 136, 140–141 (illus)
nationalism 106–107, 118–119
National party 116–117
Nectanebo II 20
Nefertiti 40 (illus)
Nefertum 25
Nephthys 24
Nile river 6–7, 50–51
Nubia 34–35, 58
Nun 24
Nut 24 (illus)

Octavian 67, 68
Old Kingdom 20–21
Omdurman, Battle of 114
Opening of the Mouth ceremony 56–57
Osiris 19, 24–25 (illus)
Osman 88–89
Ottoman Empire
 Aqaba incident 120–121
 and British occupation 107
 conquering Egypt 88–89
 everyday life in 90–91
 map, 88–89
 weakening of 118–119

Palestine 132–133
peasants. *See* Fellahin
Pepy II 30
Perdiccas 62–63
Persian empire 58–59
Persian Gulf War 149

predynastic cultures 8–9
priests 56–57
Ptah 25, 57
Ptolemy Soter 61, 62–63
pyramids 22–23 (illus)

Ramses II 35, 48–49
Ramses III 35, 52–53
Rashid Rida, Muhammad 117
Re 24
red crown of Lower Egypt 15 (illus)
religion
 Akhenaton 40
 ancient Egypt 24–25, 56–57
 Coptic church 72–73
 Islam 74–75, 130–131
Rennutet 24
Reshep 33
Roman rule 68–69, 70–71
Rosetta Stone 55 (illus)

Sadat, Anwar el- 136, 144–145, 146–147
Said 102
Saite kings 58
Saladin (Salah ad Din) 81, 82–83
Saqqarah 18–19
Scorpion, King 16–17
sea people 52–53
Second Intermediate Period 32–33
Sekhmet 25
senet 45
Seth 12–13, 24–25, 33
Shani, Ismail 137
Shirkuh 81
Sinai 120–121
Six-Day War 144
Sneferu 23
sons of Horus 28–29 (illus)
sphinx 37 (illus)
step pyramid 22–23

Sudan 113, 114
Suez Canal 102–103, 127, 129, 142–143, 144
Suez crisis 142–143
Suleiman I 118–119

Taba 120–121
Tawfiq, Muhammad 104, 106, 117, 121
Tell el-Yahudiyeh 33
temples
 Hatshepsut 37
 Mentuhotep 30–31 (illus)
Thebes 30, 49
Thutmose I 35 (illus)
Thutmose II 35 (illus)
Thutmose III 35, 36–37
time measurement 47
tombs
 mastaba 18–19
 Tutankhamen 43 (illus)
Tutankhamen 35, 42–43

Upper Egypt 8
Urabi Pasha 104–105, 106–107
U.S.S.R. 141

Wafd Party 129, 138–139
white crown of Upper Egypt 15 (illus), 16
Wingate, Sir Reginald 126
Wolseley, Sir Garnet 107
women 44–45
World War I 124–125
World War II 138–139
writing 54–55

Yom Kippur War 144–145
Young, Thomas 55
Yuya 38–39

Zaghlul, Saad 126–127 (illus), 129
Zionism 132–133
Zoser 21, 22–23

Acknowledgement

The publishers of **Childcraft** gratefully acknowledge B. L. Kearley Limited and the following artists, photographers, publishers, agencies and corporations for illustrations used in this volume. All illustrations are the exclusive property of the publishers of **Childcraft** unless names are marked with an asterisk*.

Cover	Tony Herbert	72/73	Barry Wilkinson
6/7	Mark Peppé	74/75	Charles Front
8/9	Barry Wilkinson	76/77	Donald Harley
10/11	Mark Peppé	78/79	Tony Herbert
12/13	Donald Harley	80/81	Shirley Tourret
14/15	Barry Wilkinson	82/83	Shirley Tourret
16/17	Mark Peppé	84/85	Charles Front
18/19	Donald Harley	86/87	Donald Harley
20/21	Barry Wilkinson	88/89	Trevor Ridley
22/23	Mark Peppé	90/91	Tony Herbert
24/25	Mark Peppé	92/93	Charles Front
26/27	Shirley Tourret	94/95	Tony Herbert
28/29	Mark Peppé	96/97	Tony Herbert; Culver
30/31	Barry Wilkinson	98/99	Pamela Goodchild
32/33	Trevor Ridley	100/101	Tony Herbert; Richard Steedman, The Stock Market
34/35	Barry Wilkinson		
36/37	Pamela Goodchild; Erich Lessing, Art Resource; Egyptian Museum, Berlin, Germany from Art Resource	102/103	Barry Wilkinson
		104/105	Charles Front
		106/107	Charles Front
38/39	Barry Wilkinson	108/109	Tony Herbert
40/41	Barry Wilkinson; Egyptian Museum, Berlin, Germany from Gian Berto Vanni, Art Resource	110/111	Trevor Ridley
		112/113	Charles Front
		114/115	Barry Wilkinson
42/43	Mark Peppé	116/117	Barry Wilkinson
44/45	Shirley Tourret	118/119	Charles Front
46/47	Mark Peppé; The Louvre, Paris from Giraudon/Art Resource	120/121	Trevor Ridley
		122/123	Pamela Goodchild
48/49	Barry Wilkinson; Gian Berto Vanni, Art Resource	124/125	Charles Front
		126/127	Donald Harley
50/51	Mark Peppé	128/129	Trevor Ridley
52/53	Barry Wilkinson	130/131	Trevor Ridley
54/55	Mark Peppé; British Museum, London from Bridgeman Art Library/Art Resource	132/133	Trevor Ridley
		134/135	Barry Wilkinson
		136/137	Charles Front
56/57	Mark Peppé	138/139	Donald Harley
58/59	Pamela Goodchild	140/141	Tony Herbert; AP/Wide World
60/61	Barry Wilkinson	142/143	Trevor Ridley
62/63	Barry Wilkinson	144/145	Trevor Ridley
64/65	Mark Peppé	146/147	Tony Herbert
66/67	Pamela Goodchild	148/149	Barry Wilkinson
68/69	Mark Peppé; Gian Berto Vanni, Art Resource	150/151	Donald Harley
		152/153	Egyptian Film Centre; Sygma; J. H. Morris, Panos Pictures
70/71	Mark Peppé		

Locust Grove Elementary
31230 Constitution Hwy
Locust Grove, VA 22508